If God Is...

"I found myself re-examining each *If God Is...* poem in depth. To have read several at once would have robbed me of vivid images that came with meditation. Warren Molton's personal musings and rich imagery sometimes filled a day with my own wonderment, othertimes hit me with an 'Aha' right between the eyes. Theology comes in what is seen, heard, felt. Simple acts become sacred 'If God is.'

"I like the possibilities for the poems — read the meditations first, read the poems first, use them to center a group examining their own lives, use them as a springboard for journaling or poetry of your own. If God Is as multifaceted as Warren suggests here, the personal reflections are endless.

> —**Virginia Fortner, Ph.D.**, writer, educational consultant, travel-study guide, lifelong reader

"Metaphors are essential if one is to speak of God. Ultimate Mystery defies all attempts at definition. Thus one is compelled to resort to the use of metaphor. "God is like," we say, and propose a comparison that is intentionally helpful, though inevitably less than perfect.

Molton's book hits the target straight on! His *If God Is...* should be required reading for every spiritual pilgrim — for all of us who are searching for a better understanding of God. The poems could easily stand alone, challenging the reader to think creatively. But there is more! Molton has provided an intriguing commentary on each poem, inviting us to enter into the mind and experience of the poet.

I like this book. So will you. I have my favorite poems. So will you. Each poem and commentary dares us to dig more deeply into the mystery of life, death, and the enigmatic presence of God."

> —**Harris Parker**, Professor Emeritus of Religion,
> Columbia College

"Warren Molton is a rare writer — with the mind of a theologian, the heart of a seeker and the soul of a poet. He brings all of this together in this splendid volume — where Christian hope and his talent as a therapist intermingle as countless gems to be pondered. This is a book to be cherished as the harvest of a lifetime."

> —**Rev. W. Paul Jones**, Trappist hermit, author of *The Art of Spiritual Direction* and *Teaching the Dead Bird to Sing*

"I have long been an admirer of Warren Lane Molton's tightly woven and carefully crafted poetry, and the offerings in this new book continue to delight me. However, Molton's poems here are accompanied by intriguing and often intensely biographical prose meditations which more than double the effectiveness and value of these daily readings. Molton's way with words is to explore the profound places of his own self — his memories and hopes, his dreams, fears and loves and thus this work is highly personal. Yet, at the same time, Molton's explorations almost unfailingly touch and move the one who reads, and the deeper inward he probes, the further outward he reaches. I am grateful for this remarkable book, and commend it with enthusiasm to all 'Spiritual Pilgrims.'"

—**Rev. Dr. J. Barrie Shepherd**, Retired Senior Minister of
historic First Presbyterian Church in New York

"These prayer poems are for the bruised soul, one whose "voices wrangle in the wind" with God, one whose search for peace is continuous . . . the hopeful cynic."

—**Steven Douglas Walker, Ph.D.**, Professor,
California State University, Fresno

"Warren's writing style is superb and uncommon by today's standards. He has obviously hand-carved every word and phrase to produce a dynamic set of poetic masterpieces. The poems can be provocative and display the gritty substance of life or draw one into a delicately crafted metaphor. They have the power and grace to address these contemporary, questioning times. Mixing poems about life with prose about the author's experience as man gives this work a life of its own.

"Perhaps, most importantly, I have spent time with *If God Is....* It has become my quiet companion. Those who want to detect the reality of God's presence could form a similar easygoing relationship with this book. Eventually, one starts to realize, 'If the author can open so many windows with a view of God, then surely, I can open some of my own.'"

—**Chad Simmons**, author of *Business Valuation Bluebook* and
The Anonymous Entrepreneur, founder of the Internet
Education Developer, Ceband, past President and CEO
of America's largest country real estate franchise system

"In metaphors and images sometimes entrancing, sometimes startling — and with apt prose commentary — poet Warren Molton illuminates traces and signs of the divine in ordinary life. A richly rewarding read."

—**Dean Peerman**, Contributing Editor, *Christian Century*

"In this delicately nuanced collection of his poems, Warren Molton plumbs dire doubt and the limits of faith, each one as movingly and poignantly as the other. A far from easy thing to do, he carries his readers into his own experience, offers them a glimpse of a great soul at work and provisions them with concrete, realistic and highly effective poetic images. The poems are clever, humorous and profound at one and the same time. This is a work to be savored, not simply read."

—**Rev. Dr. James A. Carpenter**, Professor Emeritus of
Theology, New York's General Theological Seminary

"Dr. Molton offers a splendid guide to creating your own spiritual reality through meditation and poetry. His medium is metaphor — a powerful tool to teach and enlighten — and this book is a work of art from a master craftsman. I highly recommend *If God Is...* — a must-read for every Spiritual Pilgrim."

—**Robert L. Price**, CEO, Reliable Investments, Inc.

"It soars! In a time of severe didacticism and pungent prejudices, Warren Molton's divine and defined collection *If God Is...* is wide-winged freedom of man's options to faith."

—**Larry Racunas**, poet

"In *If God Is...* Warren Molton amuses, enlightens, and touches us with his daringly original poetry. Imagine beginning a poem with the words, 'If God Is This Bonsai Tree,' or 'If God Is the Great Lollapalooza'? Where would you go from there?!

"No problem for Molton. He delights in following such opening lines with surprising twists, unexpected perceptions, and imaginative suggestions. We enjoy watching him effortlessly juggle his poetic words, but we are also moved by his underlying seriousness; his strikingly creative insights into the heart of the spiritual journey.

"I urge you to discover the genuine pleasure of immersing yourself in these playful passionate poems."

—**David Barstow**, Editor and Publisher of *Pilgrimage:
Reflections on the Human Journey*

If God Is...

A Poetic Search for God Within

Warren Lane Molton

FOREST OF PEACE
Publishing

Suppliers for the Spiritual Pilgrim
Leavenworth, KS

If God Is...

copyright © 2002, by Warren Molton

Library of Congress Cataloging-in-Publication Data

Molton, Warren Lane.
    If God is—: a poetic search for God within / Warren Lane Molton.
        p. cm.
Includes bibliographical references.
    ISBN 0-939516-65-9
    1. Meditations. 2. God—Poetry. 3. Christian poetry, American. I.
Title.
    BV4832.3 .M65 2002
    242—dc21

                                        2002013271

printed by
Hall Commercial Printing
Topeka, KS 66608-0007

published by
Forest of Peace Publishing, Inc.
PO Box 269
Leavenworth, KS 66048-0269 USA
1-800-659-3227
www.forestofpeace.com

1st printing: September 2002

To
Mary Dian

Contents

Epigraphs

The greatest thing by far is to be a master of metaphor.
It is the one thing that cannot be learned from others.
From metaphor we can best get hold of something new.

—Aristotle

The metaphor is probably the most fertile power possessed by man.

—Jose Ortega y Gasset

The impulse basic to all poetry is to say one thing in terms of another.

—Robert Frost

We live in two landscapes ... one that's eternal and divine, and one
that's just the back yard.

—Charles Wright

God's hands are literal, ours are metaphorical. God is reality — we
are metaphor.

—Karl Barth

Actually there is no such thing as seeing God,
for there is nothing in which he could not be found.

—Martin Buber

And this our life exempt from public haunt,
Finds tongues in trees, books in running brooks,
Sermons in stones, and good in everything.

—Shakespeare

Again the sun!
anew each day; and new and new and new,
that comes into and steadies my soul.

—Marianne Moore

To see the world in a grain of sand,
And heaven in a wild flower,
Hold infinity in the palm of your hand
And eternity in an hour.

—William Blake

So, waiting, I have won from you the end:
God's presence in each element.

                                        — Goethe

  A primrose by the river's brim
  A yellow primrose was to him
  And it was nothing more.

                                        —Wordsworth

  — until everything
  was rainbow, rainbow, rainbow!
  And I let the fish go.

                                        —Elizabeth Bishop

The eye with which I see God is the same eye with which God sees me.

                                        —Meister Eckhart

The IT is the eternal chrysalis, the THOU the eternal butterfly.

                                        —Martin Buber

  Tell the Truth but tell it slant.

                                        —Emily Dickinson

The seat of the soul is where the inner world and the outer world meet.

                                        —Novalis

One does not become enlightened by imagining figures of light,
but by making the darkness conscious.

                                        —Carl Jung

Whether we shift God's position, whether He is the God within, or
the God absolutely outside and above, or the God below as the
ground of being, or the God among wherever two or three are
gathered, or whether we are all in God and can never despite our
frenzied exercises be lost to Him — wherever we would assign Him
His place, the religious moment is in experience and that experience
takes place in the psyche.

                                        —James Hillman

When I was training at Ft. Benning to become an infantry officer, our great, black, warrior sergeant from WWII said, as we began night training, "Now men, if you can't see your target very well, look a little to the right and you'll see it just fine." Recalling his words, I wrote this quatrain:

This Is That

When old facts of faith seem fictional at best,
And ritual feels rational for all the rest,
And mystical turns magical to pass its test,
The best hope at the core is metaphor.

—Warren Molton

Religion is not a substitute for life, but rather the symbolic expression of the process of integrating the Self into a life lived in relation to the unconscious and to others.

—Ann Ulanov

I Find You Everywhere

I find You everywhere and in all things
and love You the way one loves a brother;
in small things You wait like seed in the sun
and in the large You generously give Yourself away.

This is the miraculous interplay of forces of creation
that serve through all things in this way:
germinating in roots, waiting expectantly in trunks
and in treetops bursting forth like resurrection.

—Rainer Maria Rilke, as translated by
Helga Beuing and Warren Molton

Note

Since I am committed to inclusive language, and because the gender problems of these poems seemed to have no elegant solution, I often chose somewhat randomly to mix the masculine and the feminine among the poems requiring gender pointings. Readers should feel as free to make their own pronoun choices in reading as I did in writing; and perhaps we will agree that whatever our choices, gender pronouns, however good our intentions, can still render such a brittleness to our images of God.

Preface

I have written poems most of my life. In college I discovered the great metaphysical poets: Donne, Herbert, Vaughn and others, many of whom were also clergy, who seemed to work out their soul struggle in their poems. I found poetry to be a good way to do insearch, meditation and prayer. In my own life, writing poetry has become an essential part of my dialogue with the Holy. Some prayer-poems, like dreams, are often only the "You Are Here" found on locator maps. Others awaken me, and often turn me toward a new faith experience.

These poems began when I was having difficulty finding God anywhere. Suddenly, with that probing phrase *If God Is*, I began to see God everywhere. Remembering the biblical images of shepherd, water of life, rock, door, lamb and others, I allowed the metaphors, no matter how absurd, to address me. This collection represents those that rose to the top when I chose my favorites.

So, despite all the caveats regarding the seduction of metaphor, I go to the place of these poems like a child wanting a favorite ghost story told yet again, fearful but still alive with curiosity. "Maybe this time..." and sure enough! Then it is over and I am already wondering about the next time. It is like an obsession. But did not Saint Paul in a letter to Timothy exhort us to "Pray without ceasing?" These poems of God in metaphor call me with that same insistent, urgent voice.

I have a small collection of kaleidoscopes, all of which have their own special glass fragments that make up the images — all except for one, which creates images from the surrounding environment. As I move that kaleidoscope from view to view, it blends objects and colors into spectacular patterns of startling imagery. This is a master metaphor of my search for the presence of God among us.

Meister Eckhart said, "The eye with which I see God is the same eye with which God sees me." Yet, even in the face of such a moving image, I even now often feel like I did as a child, when I covered my eyes, thinking that because I could not see, I could not be seen, and so attempt to hide in my own darkness. These poems seek light that does not depend on eyes.

Most of the poems have appeared in a variety of venues. The meditations have not. They were written as companion pieces for the poems. Some pairs seem to me as close as lovers, others are good friends, and a few but nodding acquaintances passing quickly on the street. Still, I hope you will find them all companionable, and that they will lead, with insight and inspiration, toward the ongoing creation of a defining personal inner life with God.

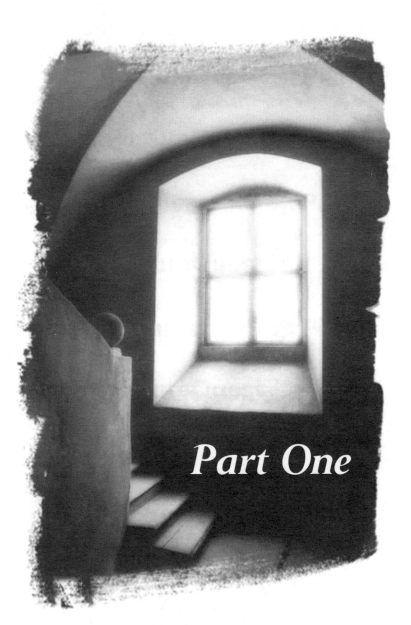

Part One

If God Is a Circle

If God is a circle
  whose center is everywhere,
  the saint dwells at the center
  and guards the well
  from which the water of all life flows,
  plants the garden that surrounds the well,
  tends the trees of life and love;
  while the poet lives at the edge of the circle,
  moving back and forth
  from the world to the well,
  troubling the saint with questions
  and filling his pitcher with water
  for the world left at the edge;
  and the people say how sweet the water is,
  how cold, how fresh and clear.
Then,
  on some fateful night or day,
  when the moon is blood
  or the sun is in eclipse,
  the water turns to wine,
  and the poet calls the saint
  away from guarding the well;
  and they drink and dance with the people
  who laugh and cry out words
  of thanksgiving and praise;
  yet, like children before sleep,
  their ecstasy turns to anger
  as they hang the poet upon a tree
  while the saint is taken to his well
  and drowned,
  just as some pilgrim saint
  comes down from the hills
  to clear the well once more
  and a wandering poet arrives
  with a new wineskin.

> If it be true that God is a circle whose center is everywhere, the saint moves to the center, the poet and artist to the ring where everything comes round again.
>
> —William Butler Yeats

The circle is our most engaging geometric figure. We find it early, up close in eyes and breasts, then away in sun and moon. Without beginning or end, like a ring it moves from symbol and sign to paradigm of God in our mind's eye for the holy.

The Greeks fixed the circle's eternity in their symbol of the uroborus, a snake swallowing its tail. Native Americans keep the circle in camp, teepee and the way they sit in community. The Chinese enclose their duality of yin-and-yang in a circle divided by a sigmoid line; smaller circles in both halves symbolize the wholeness of male and female, with each carrying the presence of the other as dark or light.

As the circle stands for transcendence, the square represents humans and earth. The notion of "squaring the circle" is more than a geometric challenge never realized; it symbolizes our human striving for the divine. The Trinity is often depicted with interlocking circles. The mandala is the great artistic effort to catch these geometric figures in what some see as a spiritual design with visual healing. Carl Jung, the great Swiss psychiatrist, painted mandalas as part of his own therapy.

Yeats follows other thinkers with his image, but he adds the dialogue between the saint, who is custodian of things holy, at the hub, and the poet and artist at the rim where all things are in flux. Hope for our evolving souls lies in that dialogue between these two within the great sphere of the holy, the circle of God.

In an essay at the end of my book of prayer poems (*Bruised Reeds,* Judson Press, 1970), I say of Yeats' image:

> The image of saint and poet should not be seen as some inimical dichotomy, which merely has the theologian stargazing and the poet ragpicking around the universe, although they surely do. Most clearly, it is a graphic metaphor for the inwardness and outwardness of reality in its further existence. The saint-poet is possible in each person's idioverse and is necessary in the universe of mankind's experience. Saint-poet and prayer-poem are one.

If God Is My Ivied Wall

If God is my ivied wall,
  gray in winter,
  when laminating ice and snow
  stick against the stone
  and a pale sun
  luminates the trail
  of leaves that keep lifting
  until they now hang
  out along the top
  like bewildered green snakes;
Then,
  we have arrived here
  together, God,
  where I too ran out of wall,
  swaying in my soul's vertigo
  and searching for a firm next rock
  on which to land
  and gain a purchase
  for the last leg of a climb
  we began so long ago
  on what then seemed to me
  to be solid ground;
But now —
  and I can take a dare —
  are you suggesting
  that I must climb solely
  on the strength of the vine
  into thin air?

My ivied wall is really an ivied wooden fence, but with imagination it could be the stone retaining wall I built across the yard of our first home in Connecticut years ago. I caught this poem in midsummer in our garden while my eyes recovered from surgery after a detached retina peeled off like a window shade coming down. One eye required scalpel, the other laser. So, I was out of season, out of focus and out of spiritual fuel as my blurred vision gave me winter and wall.

Then I saw the green tendrils dancing along the top of the fence, hanging out with no place to get a grip, trusting the vines clinging to the wall, allowing them to climb beyond certainty. The image was an echo of my condition: unanchored, off-balance, yet moving to some faith notes deep within.

It is reassuring to find a metaphor that speaks clearly to where I am, like a dream that says squarely, "You are this" — a metaphor that flashes on the inward eye of trust when the outer vision fails with no promise of better times ahead. Yet it is such a fragile image, not even animal with feelings or mineral with hardness, just watery vegetable cells with chlorophyll, swaying in the breeze and running out of wall.

Later, my neighbor over the fence, with his fill of ivy, stripped his down and some of my tendrils also fell, themselves victims of a peeling-off. But the metaphor lives and reminds me of the only thing I truly have — small cling-roots buried in God, who for one morning was an ivied wall holding up my tender vine, still reaching upward, past knowing. A green faith was still rising.

If God Is This Winter Wheat

If God is this winter wheat
    whose seed slept
    under snow just months ago,
    awaiting still another awakening,
    and now stands raised yet deep-rooted
    on heads-up stalks
    billowing in the wind
    like the sea
    that once labored here;
If God is this winter wheat
    flooding these plains
    and rolling away from me
    as far as I can see,
    even to that distance only
    seen beyond sight,
    that further view of faith;
If God is this winter wheat,
    I wave and beckon
    into the fields threshers
    arriving to harvest this God,
    whose body will be broken
    to become bread of life
    for the bellies of her world,
    even as some of us
    eat her bitter chaff of sacrifice
    to fuel our souls.

Years ago in Korea, I saw farmers threshing rice spread over straw mats to separate grain from husk, one for human consumption and the other, true to Scripture, "chaff which the wind driveth away." In the great Midwest wheat belt, the chaff is used as bulk in livestock feed.

It is hard for Christians to imagine filling our bellies with chaff while others eat bread. After all, our Lord called himself the "bread of life." Later, he took bread and broke it and gave it to his disciples, saying, "Take, eat, this is my body broken for you." No chaff bread mentioned here!

Still, the poem not only suggests we feed our bread to others for their bodies' sake, but expects chaff to feed our souls. There are times when we need the special, hard, bitter taste of chaff, knowing that we elected to give away the best, while realizing that the worst would be all that's left. Sometimes we need to make that choice. We need to be last, eating leftovers of husk and chaff. Such a fate is not very appealing, but can be the Jesus-way of sacrifice.

When I was a child, our church building barely escaped destruction by fire. The next Sunday our pastor said in his sermon on stewardship, "If this splendid edifice burned to the ground, my first call would be for a sacrificial offering for the work of our missionaries in Africa." This from a great pulpit to a huge white congregation in Georgia in the 1940s, with a black ghetto only blocks away. Still, he meant it. Give the bread away. We would need to taste the ashes a while longer. When there is no sacrifice, the faithful perish.

During the Civil Rights Movement and the Vietnam protest days, when nonbelievers and believers of all stripes worked together for common goals, and some of us needed quite simply to define ourselves, this saying was going around: A Christian is one beggar telling another beggar where to find food.

During the Depression, beggars often stopped at our door asking for food. My mother never refused them, even if her own larder was low. If they stopped at mealtime, she invited them to our table to eat with our family of six. Later, I read somewhere that during those days certain homes were "marked" so beggars would know whom to ask. I hope our house was one of them.

The widow in Jesus' parable gave beyond tithe, beyond sacrifice. She gave all she had. Since her body still required food, she might have eaten chaff, and fed her soul.

If God Is a Diviner

If God is a diviner
    teasing like a water witch,
    dowsing the inner dark
    with her witch hazel switch
    to find water beneath dry ground;
Then,
    perhaps she can divine
    my wellspring with her wand,
    find the vein
    that coils and creeps
    in the eternal deep
    where only nature can find nature
    and only the holy meets soul,
    and I can again be certain of her
    as an old rock knows its underwetness,
    an empty womb believes in sudden fruit,
    and the dark moon expects light
    each night . . .
    and a fountain will begin in me
    as sweat,
    and I shall begin to dig.

Divining, witching and dowsing are ways to describe the ancient practice of searching with a branch for water, lost or undiscovered objects, directions on a map or even covered and forgotten graves. There is little that a dowser will not try to locate. People scoff, but they keep offering as proof their often amazing results. An old dowser said, "It's another one of those believing things."

Grasping the Y-shaped branch with both hands, the diviner goes forth scanning the ground as confidently as the youngster enters the park after the carnival crowd is gone, sure he will find coins or rings lost in the grass or sawdust. As a child, I watched a dowser find the exact spot for a farmer's new well. There was no air of magic or mystery, and no one seemed surprised when it worked.

One of the oldest mysteries we ponder is the possibility that a divine being knows us and is searching us for expressions of devotion, drawing out deeds of service and sacrifice. This poem employs the metaphor of a diviner searching for water pooled or flowing underneath. The water begins modestly.

Years ago I stood with some two dozen soldiers in a Quonset hut in Korea on a Sunday morning after Saturday night's beer blast. My invocation came almost mindlessly, given to me like a dream as I opened our worship service. "O God," I said,

> If your will is water
> And earth is me,
> Then find my well
> And make a sea.

Although an English major, I overlooked the lapsed grammar, as I spoke lines imposed on me. I paused and repeated them. Then again, as though I could not move on. And yet once more, hypnotized by their seeming possibility for invoking a mighty descent of the Spirit through the sour air of our improvised chapel. I was a twenty-seven-year-old chaplain who believed God was there somewhere, and I wanted my men to be found able to live their faith abundantly in an awful time.

Later, my assistant, one clever young corporal, himself considering seminary, and never one to stand on protocol with his chaplain, teased me as he wondered if the present monsoon rains with their sudden floods had also carried me away with my ambitious prayer that kept falling on their heads. Then he laughed and added almost under his breath, "Or was it the thought of all that beer last night?" He was reading Tillich and said it was his job to keep me grounded — part diviner, scanning for truth; part trickster, scoffing at my simple trust.

If God Is Noticeably Absent

If God is noticeably absent:
    sunrise, sunset, eclipse,
    seen twice,
    coming and going,
    then gone
    up, up and away,
    everywhere at birth,
    nowhere at the death
    of his battered son,
    over the rainbow
    but not in the hurricane,
    in church
    but not with Adam
    in the packing crate
    over the grate
    on the corner,
    at the wedding
    but not the divorce;
Then,
    perhaps I shall never find him
    since he is so withdrawn,
    nor he me if I too have time
    to hide from all that's wrong,
    while he is gone.

Whenever I get caught in my anger or grief over an absent God, I know again that I am seized by one of the two greatest concerns of the human spirit. They have plagued us for as long as we have reflected upon anything: Is there a mind ordering reality? And what do we do with the myriad problems surrounding the question of good and evil?

Of the first, the reality we know is so awesome it seems certain to be in the hands of a benevolent creator. Second, if that is true, why is not our experience of good and evil rational and consistent? Good should beget good, and evil should beget evil. Whereas, often good fails and evil prospers. The dilemma is ancient, a satisfying answer unlikely.

The story of Job wrestles with this issue. The question is answered arbitrarily with God asking, "Who are you to question the mysteries of God?" So even when we ask that most troubling question, God is in effect absent, not present to our condition. It feels a little like a bright, honestly confused child asking the parent "Why?" regarding a parental decision, and getting the answer "Because I said so." Even in that desperate moment we get a vast silence.

The poem offers no answers but at least an alternative perspective: Namely, when God seems to be absent from "all that's wrong in the world," perhaps I am too. When God gave us free will, God also gave that same autonomy to all of "nature." What triggers tragic action in a person or the elements? Perhaps it is time to quit blaming an absent God. The poem suggests we might ask, "Where am I in this tragedy? What could I have done? What might I now do instead of faulting God? Am I hiding out, determined to remain innocent? Never mind God, where were Christians at the Holocaust?" Jesus was a Jew and would have been dragged off to the camps and ovens. His disciples slept through his agonizing experience in Gethsemane and fled from his crucifixion.

Perhaps we use God's absence as our excuse to be blameless in the face of evil. Perhaps God is still calling to us as in the Garden of Eden, "Adam, Eve, where are *you*?"

Hiding? Hiding? Still hiding out?

If God Is a Gardener

If God is a gardener
    with a brown thumb
    like mine, and can be
    left numb
    by the raw will and chance
    of nature, yet stunned
    by the stark dance
    of the butterfly flame
    and the timeless burn of a star;
If God can plant and prune
    and let life die
    and still let me ask why
    beyond all knowing;
If God can keep growing
    with me, can be caring
    as I have had to learn to be;
If God can believe in me
    as I keep deciding to believe in God
    and let me be guiltless
    in doing this precious
    uninvited life of mine
    in my own divine way,
    and still love me, at least
    as well as my mother did;
Then perhaps,
    and only perhaps,
    all I am becoming
    in this dear Eden of earth
    will somehow be quite enough
    to get me out of here
    into all of her.

In Christian Scriptures there are two great gardens: the Garden of Eden and the Garden of Gethsemane. Eden represents Paradise found, then lost. Gethsemane may be seen as Paradise regained. In Gethsemane, the Son of the Gardener wrestles with his soul and begs, "Let this cup pass," then rises from his prayer resolved to surrender his life in service to God's failed creation, humankind.

"Thy will be done" spoken by Jesus stands in sharp contrast to the "My will be done" attitude of Adam and Eve in Eden. In both gardens the Gardener is key to the meaning of each message. In each case God calls for obedience. God's will is refused in Eden and respected in Gethsemane. Adam and Eve are abandoned, and even Jesus, after obeying, cries from his cross, "My God, my God, why have you forsaken me?"

The poet in this poem is willing to share life's gardening with God if God is willing to strike a bargain. Namely, the poet accepts the often absurd realities and moments of meaninglessness, retaining the right to ask why. When life makes no sense, the poet and God will continue to accept, trust and love each other. "Then perhaps, and only perhaps," the poet can exit the garden, this time into the full presence of God.

Yet again, this time, the gender changes. Women were always such a presence in Jesus' life, and especially toward the end. The Marys and Salome gathered at the foot of the cross along with "many other women" who had come with him to Jerusalem. After he died, women brought spices and perfumes to anoint his body. Later, they stood vigil to see where the Romans buried him. It was again the women who arrived early at the tomb on Sunday morning. And Jesus appeared first to a woman after his resurrection. Not Andrew, the first one called to be a disciple. Not John the Beloved. Not Peter the Rock. Mary Magdalene was *chosen* as the first one to see the Risen Christ. Hence, it seemed especially appropriate with this poem that the gender of the Gardener change. Can we for a moment imagine exiting into the arms of the Great Mother of creation and nurture?

If God Is the God of Aliens

If God is the God of aliens
    firmly planted here
    and everywhere out there,
    then all we need to do is wait
    for him to get us together,
    because, after all, we are family,
    and they are just his other family,
    perhaps not even mentioned
    in his will but who could nevertheless
    show up for the reading,
    looking nothing like the rest
    of us in size, shape, language
    and perhaps, God forbid,
    even a different color
    yet
    still his,
    and now ours to get to know
    as we hear intoned to the family
    met for our inheritance: "By this
    shall everyone know who you are,
    that you love one another."
What did you say?
Why is God's will being read, anyway?
Good news has it that one
    of the Godhead died trying
    to get us aliens together,
    remember?
Everything since is only
    our reading of his will.

The prophet Micah asks and answers that most haunting question, "What does the Lord require of you, but to act justly, love mercy and walk humbly with your God?" This appears clear enough. Then we ask, justice regarding what standard? Mercy for whom and for how long? Exactly what is a humble walk? And the greatest mystery of all: Just who is "your" God? I enjoyed Golda Meir's answer when asked if she thought the Jews were God's chosen people; she said, "Without oil?"

Carl Jung, who came from a great line of clergy, said Christianity often seems too concerned about right and wrong, and good and evil, and not enough about sense and nonsense. This changes from person to person, place to place and age to age. But if God's Will and Good Sense are moving in parallel along the same timeline, both are evolving so that Jung's admonition bears attention. This from a man who also said that his relationship to God was always the most important relationship of his life.

When I look for one word to guide my thinking about God's will, the most useful for me is *inclusive*. Jesus calls us to an open, expansive, embracing God. When he was asked for the greatest commandment, he said, "Love the Lord your God with all your heart, mind, soul and strength, and your neighbor as yourself." When I was a boy in Sunday School, that got simplified to: God first, others second, me last. Later, this verse became the heart of my faith when I decided that Jesus, a real pragmatist here, was turning that sequence around and saying: "You know how much you love yourself? Well, love your neighbor and love God the same way, with all your heart, mind, soul and strength." Start where you are.

A healthy love for oneself is a major task in psychotherapy. As a pastoral counselor, I work daily with those who are trying to recover from experiences and relationships that denigrated them. Healthy love for self, as Jesus says, is where we start loving others and God. The Gospel is about love, starting with ourselves and reaching out to everyone everywhere, regardless — all the way to God.

If God Is a Snowflake

If God is a snowflake,
    I am a child
    leaving Eucharist
    this Christmas Eve,
    receiving God
    on my tongue
    cold
    as I had boldly
    taken the wafer
    of God's son,
    and deep within
    I hear again,
    Take, eat,
    as though this too
    were his body
    descending
    now to me
    in fragments
    of broken light
    flickering out
    of my winter dark
    into his glistening
    natal night.

Late one Christmas Eve I walked out the door of the sanctuary into the first flakes of a midnight snowfall. Only minutes earlier I had opened my mouth at the altar to receive the coin of the Christian realm emblazoned with the death-cross of its King, of whom we could sing, "And he shall reign forever and ever." With this bread of life came the chalice of wine recalling the faithful to a new covenant written in his blood.

The huge wet flakes fell slowly, softly, as though each unique crystal was intended for one special person. Imprinted in the heavens, they fell to us on earth, leaving the crib of the child as his children walking into darkness surprised by light. Without a thought I raised my head and opened my mouth once more that night to receive Eucharist.

Since that night I do not easily find my way to the altar on Christmas Eve. Something intimate happened to me that night, something eternal, final. It was as though for the first time I had somehow experienced my own "last supper."

That Christmas night, after many years as a pastor giving and receiving the wafer and wine, the new covenant dawned, arriving with a new experience of my own soul's need. Somehow with those cold, descending flakes dissolving on my tongue, water into wine, I felt a truly sacramental movement of the Christ Child's presence, arriving with the innocence of childhood upon the tongue of this lost child following Christ's star.

If God Is This Seeming Perfect Rose

If God is this seeming perfect rose,
    pose of sweet petals,
    pitched and whirling
    out of an infinite regression
    into this fragile time,
    choosing red,
    red above all else now
    red rising out of root and thorn;
Then,
    I who mourned her passing,
    sing now,
    as she lifts and flowers,
    drinking deeply of dark and light
    in sight of me
    that I, seeing, may believe
    her flowering,
    and praising bud and bloom
    might not again refuse this God
    come now to my dear garden
    wearing sign and symbol
    of my soul.

Gertrude Stein said, "A rose is a rose is a rose," suggesting that a rose is its own ultimate statement that cannot be improved upon. Such a perfect thing defies description, so that if asked to describe it, we ourselves might indeed stammer those very words. Now, since Gertrude, we have a ready response to a request for any obvious description.

The rose represents heavenly perfection and earthly passion. As bud and blossom, it summons both male and female imagery. It is the lotus of the Western World, suggesting completion, mystery, center of life. It represents the martyr's blood. It signifies virgin purity. It is the flower of Christ.

When I was a child in the South, we had a housekeeper named Rose. When I asked her why, she said, "Because my mama wanted to." When I innocently said that I had never seen a black rose, she wisely asked, "You ever see a beautiful rose?" When I said yes, she triumphantly said, "I'm named for that one."

Years later in our community rose garden at Loose Park, I saw a Mister Lincoln Rose for the first time. It stood tall and majestic with a single bloom at the tip of its great stem. Its hue was such a deep, dark crimson. I remembered Rose from childhood and felt moved once more by her gentle wisdom.

The English poet Coleridge offers us this: "Suppose you dream that God appears to you and speaks to you of the deep truths of your life. And just before God departs he places a rose in your hand. Then you awaken to find you are still holding that rose. Ah, what then?"

I never think of this stunning image without being touched by its power. Coleridge asks us to ponder this talisman symbol of God's visitation, a sure witness that God has addressed us personally and left evidence.

Who or what is your rose that speaks to you of God's presence in your life? Ultimately, for many of us it is the Christ, whom God leaves in our hands.

If God Is Even Somehow My Song

If God is even somehow my song,
    as in the childish poems I sang
    and the poems I left behind
    in the bright woods budding
    like Christmas lights in April;

If God is even somehow my song,
    as in the poems I composed and quickly forgot
    with the sudden rising of twin eagles
    from their pinnacle pine,
    lifting away like a ransom for me
    toward the great snow-geese marsh;

If God is even somehow my song,
    as in the poems I scribble down
    or the ones I leave printed
    in the sand as gulls and pipers
    scatter before me alongside
    the incoming tide;

If God is somehow my song,
    even in the dream-poems
    I wake from with my heart breaking
    and in tears for their missed, lost,
    sleeping elegance, now homely and naive
    in the naked morning light,

Then,
    I must keep wrestling with the Word
    if I am to find my words,
    and listening for God's song
    if I am to sing.

The late John Ciardi, one of our best contemporary poets, said that when he traveled by car he liked to eat at truck stops. It seemed to him that on almost every occasion when asked what he did and he said he was a poet, the trucker would open his wallet and say, "I've been carrying this poem for years. Whatta ya think...?" Usually it was one the driver had clipped or copied, but sometimes it was the author who was offering the poem. This led Ciardi to wonder if we all carry a poem that speaks to us of some special feeling or relationship or experience.

For most people, poetry suggests the language of intimate feelings and sentiments. The poetry may be doggerel or the verse of greeting cards, but somehow poetry seems deeper, more personal, more true or loving than prose. When someone writes us a poem, it suggests special effort and feelings. We pay attention, we savor, we may even save it, treasure it and return to it again and again.

I am a member of the American Association for Poetry Therapists, which is a group of therapists committed to the use of poetry and the healing arts. The journal and meetings are designed to share and cultivate experiences that further the effort to help people heal through writing, reading and reciting poetry. There is impressive evidence that poetry can be a therapeutic enterprise.

In the Judeo-Christian tradition the great examples of this truth of poetry are the psalms, many of which are attributed to David — friend, warrior, king, lover, husband, father and poet — who seemed to compose poems out of his own deep struggles, but whose words are the spiritual lifeblood of millions over the centuries. The Twenty-Third Psalm is probably the best-known piece of literature in the entire world.

For many, as Rilke said, poetry is the natural language of the soul. Poetry is the channel between creature and Creator, a voice we find even when the Word falls silent, when even that silence is hallowed in the vessel of the poem.

In therapy, I once asked a woman to write a psalm about her child born dead. She did and brought it in to read to me. Halfway through, surprising us both, her voice quietly became a chant as her words were changed into her soul's healing cry.

Part Two

If God Is Any Great Returning

If God is any great returning,
　　a listening to some new witness
　　bidding within,
　　any hard going back
　　to where in a rootless time
　　you quit,
　　as Bonhoffer left life in New York
　　to return to his death in a Nazi prison,
　　so that now it's your turn
　　at the bitter feast of eating crow,
　　saying I'm sorry
　　to every cynical hello
　　after your selfish good-bye;
If God is any great returning,
　　your soul's yearning,
　　lonely and longing
　　for the path lost or deserted,
　　the cause dropped in its infancy
　　as too childish, too hard, too frail,
　　too sure to fail to bother,
　　but now somehow the only way
　　worthy of your life,
　　your death;
If God is any great returning,
　　and your burning soul
　　has spun your compass about
　　so that you are finally en route home
　　like the prodigal;
Then,
　　go quickly,
　　expecting to feast with the Father
　　even though your whining brother
　　may not yet dine with you
　　and in truth
　　awaits proof, even as he should,
　　that you are really home
　　for good.

There are lots of prohibitions against going back, from Lot's wife looking back with longing and turning into a pillar of salt, to the saying that Thomas Wolfe used as the title of his novel *You Can't Go Home Again*. There is a spiritual mandate in the human soul to press on. Even Jesus told his disciples that if one village rejected them, they should shake its dust off their feet and move on to the next. Life is too short to keep trying in the face of certain failure. Folk wisdom says that a neurotic is one who continues destructive behavior while expecting a different outcome. Hence, to return to a place, person, conviction or behavior after failure can seem like a death wish. Yet, in Jesus' parable about the return of the prodigal son, returning is the message for all of us — *returning* to God who waits and watches for us.

The Greek word for conversion in the New Testament is almost always translated *turn* or *turning,* moving in the opposite direction. To re-turn is to participate in the meaning of conversion even if we are going *back*. Ultimately for a believer every re-turn is a going-back-to-God moment, whether we have been away for a short time or a lifetime.

How is the verb "to return" a loving command that can change our direction, a relationship, an appetite, a commitment — something at the core of us — and so focus new life for our soul? A Church legend tells of St. Peter fleeing Rome, until he met Christ on the road and asked, "*Domine, quo vadis?*" ("Lord, where are you going?") to which Christ answered, "I am going to be crucified again." Peter, who had denied his Lord three times, returned to Rome where he was crucified head-downward.

Saint Luke, in his Gospel, says that Jesus "steadfastly set his face to go to Jerusalem." Theologian Dietrich Bonhoffer might have lived out his life writing and teaching in New York at Union Theological Seminary, where Reinhold Niebuhr had encouraged him to join the faculty. But God called him back to Germany. There, as a Christian pacifist, opposed to violence, he nevertheless joined the plot to assassinate Hitler, which failed. Bonhoffer was arrested in 1943 and hanged at Flossen on April 9, 1945, just days before his camp was liberated by the allies. His poem written in prison, which he entitled "Who Am I?" will survive as a great piece of contemporary Christian devotional literature, not because it is great poetry but because it is the soul-cry of a great man who returned home and wrote it with his life. The poem ends:

Who am I? They mock me, these lonely questions of mine.
Whoever I am, Thou knowest, O God, I am thine.

Bonhoffer returned to his country and to the Crucified Christ who ruled his life.

If God Is That Sublime Moment

If God is that sublime moment
    in the story when Jesus said,
    "And his father seeing him afar off . . ."
    which could mean, of course,
    that he had been watching every day for years,
    longing for him,
    straining to see him afar off —
    it's that afar off that moves me;

    or perhaps he only watched
    in the late afternoon,
    thinking his son might try to get home before dark,
    or early in the morning
    after pressing on all through the night,
    or at high noon
    when his father stood
    shadowless under the sun
    and remembered his son's
    innocence and sweetness;

    or perhaps it was just by chance
    he saw him
    when he looked up
    from repairing a harness
    or tying a new broom
    or from a nap in his favorite chair,
    suddenly there he was,
    his lost son
    coming home . . .

    or perhaps he only saw him
    because it was his birthday —
    his,
    not his son's —
    when his eldest,
    forgetting the persistence of an old man's dream,
    said, "Make a wish, Father,"
    and he did
    and looked up . . .
    seeing him afar off.

The story of the prodigal may be the greatest tale ever told. The younger of two sons, perhaps tired of walking in his older brother's shadow or perhaps just bored and restless, decides to leave. He does not have to run away. Indeed, he is able to depart with his inheritance, which he subsequently squanders. Finally, reduced to eating with pigs, he remembers his father and goes home. There he is extravagantly celebrated with robe and ring and a party. When the older brother complains that he stayed home and was a good son but his father never honored him this way, the father makes a simple defense: "But this my son, your brother, was lost and is found. This is a great day. Join us in celebrating his homecoming!" How many sermons have been preached on this parable!

The story has all the basic dramatic elements of great theater. Classic, moving themes drive the drama: hubris, gluttony, waste, awakening, homegoing, jealousy, celebration. The youngest is his own victim, persecutor and rescuer as he saves himself from his foolishness and goes home. The three characters who fuel the dramatic tension are good son, bad son and forgiving Father. Things could not have been right between the sons or the older would not have questioned their father's celebrating his brother's return. The youngest ate crow and returned to further rejection by his brother. We may want to fault the father for not being as demonstrative toward his eldest, but that's a long shot. This is a once-in-a-lifetime feast when the lost is found, the dead raised. Jesus' most powerful stories deal with awakening to a new consciousness — darkness into light — with celebration. Go in peace, go and rejoice, give thanks and be glad!

There are so many lessons here, truth from every perspective. But of them all, the one that moved me the most early on was the camera angle so easily lost: the father, seeing him afar off. This, I believe, is what Jesus was about — this was his soul talk. Not the goodness of the eldest nor the wickedness of the youngest. Not even that the young man woke up, went home and was rewarded. Jesus' analogy of the father is that his God is watchful, waiting, longing for us to remember and go home. "Afar off" says it all. We cannot stray so far away that, even if we lose sight of God, our God could ever lose sight of us. Hear again that astonishing image from Meister Eckhart: "The eye with which I see God is the same eye with which God sees me." Both of us, from afar: "I can't wait to see you." That good news shines in the eyes of the beholders.

If God Is This Battered Basin

If God is this battered basin
carried down the aisle
in my grandmother's hands,
towel over her arm,
walking with the singing,
"Shall we gather at the river?"
a capella in this Freewill Baptist
Church near Macon in 1934;
If God is this tin bowl
she fills from a white pitcher
while kneeling at the front pew
weeping and washing her neighbor's
calloused, hard-nail feet:
my Grandma,
with her waterfall tears tumbling
into Sister Ella's hands, cupped,
cradled to catch the Spirit;
Then,
wash me now also, God,
in this memory pan,
Grandson recalling Grandma
brought to footwashing
for who-knows-what small sins
of gossip or forgetfulness
and her persistent need
to get right with God;

wash me, who walked on without her
but always with this vision of her
doing what her Lord did,
because she hurt so
and because she and Sister Ella
needed to cry together
and embrace each other
and give each other a holy kiss
as now when Ella stands, then kneels
to wash my grandmother's feet
in their shared water,
in that battered basin
of God's love.

On the night Jesus was betrayed he took a towel and basin of water and washed his disciples' feet. After they shared bread and wine, Jesus said, "Do this in remembrance of me." For some, foot washing is a part of that remembrance. For many, it is as powerful a ceremony as the supper, gathering up another set of symbols, especially representing the side of his ministry that Jesus so poignantly exemplified, Isaiah's "suffering servant." There he was on his knees washing dusty feet. Providing water for drinking and washing was not only good hospitality in the parched lands of the East, but it was also a part of practicing one's faith. Yet for the host, washing his guests' feet was new that night, and the disciples rightly objected. If anyone was going to wash feet, they should wash his. Earlier, on the mount when Jesus was transfigured before them, the disciples wanted to build altars and remain there to worship him, but Jesus insisted they return to the valley to serve the broken people of God who were the inspiration for his beatitudes and the heart of his ministry.

The experience in my grandmother's church remains one of the moving events of my life. It is the only foot washing service I ever attended. I have, almost with tongue in cheek, suggested it to small groups in other churches, only to be met with looks of dismay or indulgent smiles. No one has yet burst out laughing.

After I decided to prepare for the ministry, I discussed the events of that Sunday with my grandmother and asked how often they included foot washing with the Lord's Supper. She was ninety-three at that time and just gazed at me from her nursing home bed as though going back to those days, then finally said, "I guess we did it whenever we thought enough of us wanted it. God knows we needed it every Sunday. But you know, one of our worst sins is laziness, and it was a lot easier to sit in the pew and let the deacons bring us those little cubes of bread and cups of grape juice." She waited. "I guess you could say we sinned by omission every Sunday at the Supper." Another pause. "Seems sad we would miss a chance like that."

She and I were quite close when I was a youngster and she lived with us for a time. Now, it was hard to leave her. We both knew this might be our last time together. I kissed her old mapped cheek and we were tearful, as she touched my hand, smiled and blessed our good-bye with, "Warren, enjoy your life, no matter what you do." The light in the room brightened as the setting sun found her windows.

If God Is This Bonsai Tree

If God is this bonsai tree,
   burnt-orange leaves
   igniting in the October sun
   of my florist's window . . .
   and here miniature
   in leaf and limb,
   trunk and root,
   marooned in a potter's dish;
If God is this ancient bonsai
   trapped like me
   in an earthen vessel,
   going through the motions
   of his seasons, sunrise-sunset,
   in his own sweet rule of time,
   dwarfed
   but ever budding, blooming toward
   an autumn burning;
Then,
   I pause
   before his emblem flame
   that God might light my soul
   like a Moses bush,
   that I might keep seasons with him
   without a doubt
   and not burn out.

Soon after the experience described in the poem, my family gave me a bonsai on my birthday — not a major anniversary but one ending in one or three, a middling day of modest gifts. So I was surprised at their extravagance. Bonsai can be quite expensive. With the tree came Darlene Dunton's *The Complete Bonsai Handbook* telling me all I needed to know about the care and feeding of bonsai. Alas, not complete enough for me. I do have a bit of a green thumb, so everyone assumed this to be a new member of our family destined to take its own auspicious place (dare I say it?) in the family tree. Bonsai are known to live for generations.

However, soon after entering my care, this bonsai began showing signs of distemper. At least that's what I called it, since all we ever had growing in our house, short of various ivy, were cats and dogs. Besides, distemper seemed not only to fit its condition but later its attitude as it refused to rally with my ministrations. I finally called the Bonsai Society of Greater Kansas City and talked with a Dr. Ty Sato, whose name and profession sounded promising. He was understanding and reassuring with his suggestions. He then referred me for a second opinion to a member named Dorothy, which in a City named Kansas sounded absolutely magical. She would surely take me to the wizard. Not to be.

Nothing availed. My tree was determined to die. I patiented it out to Gary Hartman, a real green thumb Jungian analyst, in whose care my bonsai, smitten with a Freudian death wish, finally — through no fault of Gary's — expired. Loving plants as he does, Gary mulched a proper interment.

Throughout my ordeal with this *If God Is...* metaphor, I have recalled literature of the period from J. B. Phillips' *Your God Is Too Small* to Bishop Robinson's *Honest To God* (sounding much like my plea to the tree to explain itself), on down to the "God is Dead" movement, to which I had contributed a brief article of protest — which, in turn, was published in two places with my name misspelled both times. My metaphor God died, was buried and never rose again. My green thumb browned a smidgeon. The florist failed and moved away, and I was sure I had disappointed my family. All in all, not a numinous journey with metaphor. We all have times like that with God. Some for a whole lifetime.

"Pray for us sinners now and at the hour of our death."

If God Is This Solitary Cloud

If God is this solitary cloud
    small and fragile in an empty sky
    barely shining, like tarnished silver in the sun
    under a sea-hue dome over the Atlantic,
    a mere silly sneeze of a cloud
    not bright enough to find a form
    nor brave enough to travel,
    no kin to the pillar of cloud by day
    or column of fire by night that led
    the Hebrews over the desert to Mt. Sinai —
    just sitting out there
    looking lost,
    attracting nothing I can see
    except this squadron of pelicans passing across
    and making such a flying wing line
    over me
    that my eye snaps the shot
    as though to keep it forever;
Then,
    who knows, God,
    maybe somewhere in here
    I have a negative of you
    should I ever want the photo
    for an album I am making;
    still,
    I feel somewhat foolish about it all
    embarrassed somehow,
    sad even —
    you just hanging out there like that —
    perhaps I feel a little like old Moses
    on Mt. Nebo
    must have felt
    when he, your faithful servant,
    asked to see your face,
    but you only showed him
    your backside as you passed.

I came in from the beach and wrote this poem about what happened on my walk. Then suddenly I remembered my first poetry reading. I was in the second grade at Charles H. Bruce school in Macon, Georgia. It was September and the windows were open, the air warm. I sat in the second seat of the third row. Miss Melton asked me to read a poem by Christina Rossetti. I was surprised but pleased. Suddenly my heart raced as I began, stumbling on the word "trembling" as I read these lines:

> Who has seen the wind?
> Neither I nor you:
> But when the leaves hang trembling,
> The wind is passing through.
>
> Who has seen the wind?
> Neither you nor I:
> But when the trees bow down their heads
> The wind is passing by.

Something deep changed in me that day. With the reading, poems were separated from my mother. They had a life of their own. They were alive in the world like other people's children who were my friends. Jesus and my mother and I were still together, but poems had been set free. The world of words was wonderfully different. But I could tell my mother only that I had been called on in class to read. Now, writing these lines, new words come uninvited like a break-in:

> Who has seen God?
> No one is what I hear:
> But if I watch with inward eye
> I see God drawing near.

Who has seen God? Who indeed? Literally, no one. Metaphorically, everyone. Martin Buber said, "Actually there is no such thing as seeing God, for there is nothing in which God could not be found." And one of Rilke's poems begins, "I find You everywhere and in all things." They disagree in order to agree. Mystics aspire to the *Imago Dei* (Image of God) experience. We should be encouraged in our search for God.

God knows it's hard to stay on the path. Still, I try. These poems are one way I keep searching. Then comes the question, "So what?" I can only keep writing what I saw, and then see where it goes. Sometimes, it's nowhere. But if you keep your eyes open, or closed if you prefer, you never know what you might see. This time, I saw this solitary, sort of silly cloud, and look where it took me. Maybe it's not much, but it's more of God than I had before and also more of me. Better luck next time? Maybe. I'll just have to wait. And see.

If God Is a Poet

If God is a poet,
    he must have written
    his first poem about creation
    before creating it
    and got everything down
    perfectly backwards with
    no sin, no pain, no death,
    and hence paradise
    with no real life to live.
Fortunately,
    the poem failed upon the page,
    and the frustration God must have felt
    with his boring humankind
    set him grieving over
    his own lack of imagination,
    until God remembered that
    he had a choice
    and in the rewrite
    turned us loose
    to choose,
    which gave God something new to do
    and someone
    to read, memorize and recite
    his collected works.

As one who has slaved over manuscripts both as author and editor demanding rewrites of myself and others, I have always found the working papers that writers save and share absolutely fascinating. To read a poem I love and cannot imagine written any other way, or to read that a favorite novelist tried twenty-three different endings to a book that I think is perfect — these possibilities still seem impossible. When I read the first draft of Elizabeth Bishop's poem *One Art*, then remembered the version that I love, I was left wondering how she ever arrived at the final draft over which she exulted, "Yes!" But how great that she kept at it.

A favorite rule for writers is: Just write, write, write; you can clean it up later. Find the fire and let it burn. The rewrite is a given. The passion is a gift.

Once when I was writing a piece of fiction I paused for lunch. I was slicing a tomato when my hero announced, "I wouldn't have done any of that stuff." I laughed aloud and went back to rip up the morning's work.

This poem is a playful wondering about God and God's creation. Sometimes I feel like a first draft, part of God's passion but definitely unfinished. Other times I feel like a poem overwritten into flat prose. I wonder if God ever asks of me: "How did you get here from there?" And might there be even yet another rewrite? Am I worth it? Might I like me then? Will you? Does it matter? I hope the Author stays with me, doesn't doze off, trusts how I will turn out, keeps searching for the poem in the prose of me.

Once in a Thee-and-me downtime, I wrote these lines that come back to me now:

> Somewhere along this holy way
> My dear soul lost her voice,
> And all I recall to comfort me
> Is her last word, "Rejoice!"

I try to remember to do that. There is always so much for which to give thanks *now*, no matter how we turn out or what God finally finds to do with us.

If God Is This Crowing Rooster

If God is this crowing rooster
>*too near just now to my host's house*
>*at sunrise,*
>*and standing doubtless on some elevation,*
>*hen house, fence or even a watering trough,*
>*some prominence "high and lifted up" —*
>*from which to announce the sun,*
>*which by the way won't be getting up at all today,*
>*or at least nowhere near here*
>*in the storm we are promised;*

Then,
>*I would prefer he find a more gentle*
>*morning thing to do,*
>*just settle down and let my day arrive*
>*as it will, especially since I was writing*
>*till well past one*
>*and he's left me with only four hours of sleep at best,*
>*but more than that*
>*I resent his attitude, his arrogance*
>*of "this is my time, my thing, my tune*
>*and you'd just better get used to it" —*
>*a sort of "I crow or you can go" motto*
>*in great letters across his sky;*

But,
>*this Rooster-God*
>*does give me pause and make me wonder*
>*if, when Jesus told Peter that he would*
>*betray his Master three times before the cock crew,*
>*Jesus meant simply before dawn,*
>*or before God woke him up.*

Saint Peter is known as Prince of the Apostles. However we interpret the time, history and purpose of the Gospels, he appears throughout as leader. He is also one of an inner group and the mouthpiece for them all. One day Jesus asked his disciples, "Who do you say that I am?" And Peter said, "You are the Christ, son of the living God." Jesus then named him Cephas, Aramaic for Peter (Rock), and in Matthew says, "On this rock I will build my church." Whether you believe Jesus meant on Peter or Peter's confession or on both, Peter did in fact become the leader of the emerging Christian movement taking the Good News to the Gentiles all the way to Rome, where it is believed he was martyred during the days of Nero's persecution.

However, on the same night in which Jesus was betrayed, Jesus told Peter that Satan would "sift him like wheat." Then he added, "But I have prayed for you that your faith would not fail you, and when you are converted, strengthen your brothers." Then Jesus predicted that before morning, before the cock crew, Peter would deny him three times. Later that night after Jesus was taken into custody by the authorities, Luke says that Peter followed "afar off" as far as the court of the High Priest, where he stopped to warm himself with a group gathered around a fire. A servant girl, spotting Peter, accused him of also being with Jesus, which he denied. She accused him again, and again he denied it. She persisted, saying he also was a Galilean and she had seen Peter with him, and Matthew says that Peter swore and said, "I do not know the man." And immediately the cock crew.

All in one man: "You are the Christ, Son of the living God," and "I do not know the man." Confession meets conflict. Conversion confronts convenience. Crucifixion encounters comfort. Conscience meets cowardice. Oh, we could go on and on from here all the way to Christ versus Caesar — Jesus against the world. This world, our world. I've been there. Perhaps you have too. I guess we all have and will again. And what is our hope? Jesus said to Peter, "And after you are converted, strengthen your brothers" ... and sisters, we add. Conversion? This is the man of the Great Confession who led the way. Is conversion an ongoing need? Maybe. Especially *after* God wakes us up with all that crowing.

If God Is All Hammered Time

If God is all hammered time,
   rockets piercing tanks,
   rapid-fire bullets pelting flesh,
   bells briefly clapping for peace,
   sleet tapping
   a blind man's dark glasses,
   a dusting moth thumping
   inside the yellow lamp shade
   even the catching, counting,
   pouring-to-empty ancient waterwheel;
Then,
   God ticks down
   to this clock's pendulum
   swinging out,
   hanging for an instant,
   then slicing our breathed air
   back through center
   until a deep tolling
   ends our moments together
   with the softest blows of all,
   my heartbeat
   against your dear cheek.

Both of my grandfathers wielded hammers for a living. Grandpa Lane was a blacksmith and carriage maker. He took great pride in telling his grandchildren that he once built the inaugural carriage for his governor. Grandpa Molton was a master carpenter and home builder whose structures still stand after a century of battering time.

Grandpa Lane's shop smelled of coke fire and horse sweat. The clinker floor, leather harness, bellows blowing a blue-to-white-hot flame, hammer, tongs and anvil shaping all things iron, before they were dipped sizzling into the water vat, created a wizard's den and my childhood's most enchanted environment. When a horse jerked against my grandfather's arm, holding the great leg like a vice, my grandfather merely yanked back and pounded nails that held the horse's shoe.

When I was four, my older brother, Ronnie, and I stopped by Grandpa's shop to say good-bye on our way home by train. He paused at his forge, reached under his leather apron and found a dime, which he flipped through the air to me across the shop. It plinked on the cinder floor and disappeared. "Let 'er go," he laughed and flipped another. This one plunked into a tub of beer with its block of ice, which he kept with a gourd dipper for any man with a great thirst. My grandfather walked over, plunged his huge arm deep into the pungent, yeasty brew and recovered my dime. He smiled, patted me on my head, gave me the coin and said, "Bye, Preacher Boy," the nickname he gave me because I was named for a minister.

Memories of that day are full of sounds: his hammering that greeted us, the dimes plinking and plunking, his laughing and patting my head with his big hand, my heart pounding with regret as we walked away. I did not want to leave. Ronnie, ten years older, picked me up, wiped my tears and carried me to the station three blocks away, consoling me.

The earliest hammering time we know is the sound of our mother's heartbeat coming to us through the waters of her womb. It is our first measuring of anything. It is the first beat setting a rhythm to life, the ground of music and the steady sound we seek the rest of our lives among the signs of health.

Time is our most common and universal measure. Its throb is persistent, pervasive, relentless and unstoppable. If the heartbeat is the first hammering we know, how good to return again and again to its most loving chamber, the arms of love, where we listen for that primal drumbeat signaling deep union with our deepest loves. These are the bonding beats of lovers. Remember them. Seek them. Cherish them. Across time. In the echo chamber of the heart.

If God Is Love

If God is love,
  there is no place where love is not;
  and although this seems like a double negative,
  sounds like a plot, a Gordian knot,
  and is easier said than believed,
  it rings true, feels good,
  even theological as in "word of God" —
  all of that, and that's a lot.
Still, there is no place where love is not.
Yet, we live like fish
  swimming about in search of water,
  or a blind mole pressing on to find soil,
  or the olive its oil — absurd, like a bird
  flying around without a care, looking for air.
  No, love is everywhere. Yet, such a paradox!
For still, we must look for love: around the bend,
  over the rainbow, across this room or that street,
  on the other side of an argument.
Near or far, we must search for love,
  knowing that it is hard to find,
  but hardest of all when love is finally found.
For then we must cherish it,
  we must nurture it and help it grow,
  then let it go.
So, if we are born, bathed and buried
  in love, you and I have no excuse
  not to be God's lovers in the world,
  all of us all of the time, starting here and now
  by loving ourselves,
  and taking loving steps toward others,
  as holy others, and on to every living creature,
  all the way to God.
For it is with the eye of love
  that we find God,
  and the eye of love that God finds us.
What a lovely way to live,
  and, of course, the only way to die.

God is love. That sublime thought is the quintessential metaphor, and this poem is like a vessel for the entire collection. If God is love and God is everywhere, then love is everywhere. All we need to do, as the Chinese ideogram for love suggests, is to breathe it into our hearts.

Even though Hebrew has a number of words used to express love, it mostly uses only one. Greek has four, but in the New Testament *agape* is most often used. It means love between God and humankind as shown ultimately in his gift of Jesus: "For God so loved the world that he gave his only begotten son...." John's Gospel makes a great love statement, as does I John 4. But, of course, St. Paul's hymn in the thirteenth chapter of I Corinthians is the noblest of all, ending: "Now abides faith, hope and love, these three; but the greatest of these is love."

Expressions of God's love are found throughout the Bible. The Shema in Deuteronomy says, "Love the Lord your God with all your heart, soul and strength," and it lies at the very heart of the Covenant. Devout Jews say the Shema twice daily. When a lawyer asked Jesus what was the greatest commandment, Jesus went straight to the Shema, then added, "...and thy neighbor as thyself," making an incredible addition. Thus, People of the Book know and believe that love is the great unifying conviction at the core of our faith. It remains the only real hope for our fractured world. Yet, so many of us live as though we do not know or care about this supreme commandment from one who lived it faithfully. We love because God first loved us.

Paul Tillich says that love is the drive towards unity of the separated. Although *eros*, the Greek word for erotic love, is not used in the New Testament, its passion for connecting is also found in the other three words for love. Every love word is about unity. Christ came to break down the walls of separation, and love is never so powerful as when it heals the most awful division. The broken are healed by love, the lost are found because of love, the estranged reconciled.

Finally, Jesus stretched, nearly to breaking, every call for love found throughout all Scriptures when he commanded us to do the ultimate. We like to think he said it expectantly, trustingly. Yet, there is the note of a plea, almost begging out of the depths of his heart, when he says: "Love your enemies." He did. Even those who slew him. We have a long way to go. There he is up ahead, beckoning...as night comes on.

If God Is This Fearful Wind

If God is this fearful wind
    spinning in from the open sea
    with a Sinai voice commanding
    our wet gray beach to batten down
    and drunken sea oats to dance
    on the dunes like dervishes gone mad;
If God is this fearful wind
    talking in tongues
    across our deck, under eaves
    and down our flutey chimney:
        Trust, but take cover,
        Believe, but button down,
        Pray, but ponder leaving;
If you, God, are this fearful wind
    howling in my soul,
    I must ride you out
    since you leave me no retreat,
    not even some neat formula to predict
    velocity, direction or possible damage;
    still,
    our voices wrangle in the wind . . .
    yours, God, and mine,
    and in our whirlwind of tongues
    I answer you:
        Remember, God,
        you are on your way
        while I must stay,
        so blow and go,
        as I await that great calm
        hiding,
        riding like a rainbow
        on your tail.

On my sixty-fifth birthday, with loved ones arriving from all over to our retreat at the beach in Charleston, South Carolina, it began to rain. After a week of sunny days, the wind was slapping rain against doors and windows. The tired jokes of Noah and the ark began. I was not amused.

Our plan was to caravan at six from Wild Dunes over the bridge to Charleston down along the Ashly River to the dinner cruise boat waiting to take thirty-six of us around the tip along the battery with its array of splendid antebellum homes, up the Cooper River past navy ships at anchor and back to dock. Deckside viewing would surely be impossible if the rain continued, and with high water predicted for the streets, well . . . it seemed bleak.

As the hour approached, we dressed for dinner, the women in their gorgeous gowns and the men fit to accompany them. The rain was going too, on and on. Finally, in a desperate gesture of phony power, I walked to the great window, raised a clenched fist and shouted, "God, stop it!" Everyone laughed. A few shouted, "Yeah, God," mocking me.

I picked up an armful of newspapers, thinking they might serve to cover our heads from door to cars, and we moved to the elevators. By the time we reached the ground just five floors below, the storm had quit. "I didn't even see the dove," someone teased. I was speechless.

We made our drive safely. The cruise was spectacular. The food was wonderful. The dancing joyous. And by eleven we were going home.

Back at the condo with all the cars parked and the last person out of our van, I was walking alone in this wonderful night toward the door when I felt the first drops. I stopped, looked up for long moments until tears and rain wet my face. "Thank you," I called.

Then an old, familiar, chiding voice inside that enjoys bursting my balloon said, "Well, I see the rain is back. What's the shelf-life of your prayer-life, Pal?" I am still working on that.

Part Three

If God Is This Rattler

If God is this rattler
　　I am stripping
　　off its skin
　　when I am ten,
　　pulling with mouse-nose
　　pliers at the hide
　　along the beads
　　of blood
　　beneath his head
　　on down each side and over a carcass
　　fit now only for a meal
　　to brag about,
　　down finally
　　to the rattling end
　　of his last shedding
　　as green flies
　　swarm
　　at the awful head
　　hammered
　　with nails
　　to my favorite tree,
Then,
　　that must be
　　why I will find
　　I can never climb
　　this tree
　　again
　　or drive nails
　　through any living bark.

When I was a boy of twelve, our father rented a farm for a year in Beach Island, South Carolina, ten miles across the border from Augusta, Georgia, where he worked for a small railroad. As a gentleman farmer, he wanted to give his wife and four sons this rural experience. It turned out to be one of the best years of my childhood.

We had it all: a horse, two mules, a cow, pigs, guineas, eighteen goats and three hives of bees. There were no powered implements. The farm included forty acres of Savannah River bottomland known to produce amazing corn crops. One spring day while my brother Ronnie was plowing, our mule, Tom, was bitten by a rattlesnake, which my brother killed. Tom also subsequently had to be shot. It was a terrible day, for I loved Tom, and had ridden him around the farm bareback with only a halter.

My brother needed a trophy, I guess, so he nailed the rattler through its head to my tree, cut a ring around its neck and skinned it bare. He dried the skin with proper oiling, and later covered a belt with the hide of the snake. Ronnie wore it proudly. I was never once jealous of the belt. I remember that he wore it off to the war.

But my tree was also lost for me. Ronnie had cut off the snake at the head and left it nailed to the tree. Those eyes watched me at any angle and every passing. Even when the head was finally buried, the tree remained haunted and I couldn't go near it. Nor could I ever hammer nails into any tree without remorse, without my mind going back all the way to Golgotha.

If God Is an Apple

If God is an apple
    and I slice it down,
    I find a heart print
    with seeds,
    and if across
    I see a star
    shining at the center
    of this fruit
    which Eve
    is said to have offered Adam
    and hence to all
    who believe the apple story;
And
    if God is this apple on my tree,
    I shall gather it myself,
    leave it whole, unsliced,
    and eat it round and round,
    eat its heart and star,
    leaving only seeds
    upon the ground,
    perhaps to start again
    some new tale
    that lets me risk
    my own
    tiny serpent
    at the core.

Such a symbol, the apple! Like a space-time traveler in a constellation of symbols, the apple visits sundry ports and finds commerce everywhere. In numerous cultures the apple is a symbol of mercy, celebration, eternal youth, totality, unity, things global, the new year, a declaration of affection for the teacher, sensual beauty, apple blossoms of fertility for the bride, whole as the heart and sliced in half as a Venus mound and symbol of lovers' bliss. In our own theology, the apple has come to represent the "forbidden fruit" picked by Eve to seduce Adam into disobedience after the serpent's assurance that no harm would come to them, doubting scholars who say it was a fig notwithstanding.

My most poignant apple moment occurred when our two older children, Stephen and Jennifer, were quite young. One afternoon they asked me to cut our only apple in half for them, and to cut it "sideways" just for fun. I was familiar with the tiny heart at the center when cut lengthwise, but we were all surprised to find the five-point star revealed with my crosscut: both hearts and stars seed-studded.

Years later, on another apple day of deep inwardness, it seemed I had to take this fruit held out to Adam or clutched in the hand of the artist's Christ Child and leave it *unsliced*. I would eat both heart and star, one taking me to the heart of temptation and the other out to the remotest star-fires, God's eyes. And with this apple I would again quicken to my own small serpent hiding within, reminding me of my dark shadow at the core seducing me to live as though God would not come walking in the cool of my day, find me naked and ask me why, if I despised innocence and demanded to eat of the tree of the knowledge of good and evil...why, why indeed, should I think that such knowledge might not also impose upon me the chance for star-crossed choices and heart-wrenching consequences?

If God Is This Fallen Sparrow

If God is this fallen sparrow,
    angelic wings windblown,
    ice-laced yet spread
    somehow as in frozen flight,
    neck broken, lights out,
    lying now below the window
    of its reflection . . . glass
    through which was darkly seen
    my world away from night chill,
    this sparrow's farther distance to go
    toward hearth fire and yule tree;
Then,
    let even this also be nativity,
    let these most common wings
    of God delivered in their streak
    toward light back to earth
    birth in us a caring
    for all those other children . . .
    everywhere since Bethlehem
    stopped cold on their way
    to Christmas.

I heard it hit the window as dusk came on. Carols were playing in our new stereo, candles were lit, a fresh fire popped in the fireplace, the pine tree's lights danced. It was the first Christmas in our new home, which we had designed with a lot of help from the developer. All was ready for our three children soon to return from a sledding party on what they fearlessly called Suicide Hill in Storrs, Connecticut, where I was a campus minister. John F. Kennedy's death had all but shredded the season, and Christmas was coming to save us all.

I knew before I turned toward the window that the knock like a knuckle rap upon the glass was a bird. We had a variety of birds in the fifty or so trees on the acre of our lot that had once been a nursery. Spottings of cardinals were rare, even announced on the local radio station. Neighbors alerted neighbors, and one friend had a convincing fake mounted with wire on a limb near her kitchen window.

I walked out into the chilly air because I had to know. This was no cardinal, only a sparrow. Then I recalled Jesus' words and felt a flashing natal presence that surprised me awake. With one quick sleight-of-hand, Jesus raised the sparrow from "you know the commonest" to "well, my heavenly Father pays attention when even this one falls." The first shall be the last and the last first. The bird fell. God saw it. Here, this night at my window. Nothing that season caught me so unaware announcing God with us. My mind took one further step to the slaughter of innocents as Herod tried to net Jesus early. Then one more, to a friend's child celebrating Christmas early because of a ravaging leukemia, and another, to all infant innocents stopped cold on their way to Christmas. "My heavenly father knows and cares," says the one who greets us with his whole new life of love again and again every Christmas.

If God Is Bored

If God is bored
    with my complaining,
    yet still listening with a listless hope,
    pondering what I seem to want,
    wondering how she can ever please me
    beyond the gifts already given
    of soul-mates and heart-mates,
    so many loving me
    beyond my cup of returning;
If God is weary of me,
    as friend of spoiled friend
    always yearning for more
    time, praise, attention,
    comparing gift to gift,
    needing nothing
    yet begging for everything;
Then,
    if I'm to believe what I am getting here,
    I may have my answer to her silence:
    it is her quiet ache to design in time
    something, anything short of laughter,
    to stop this whine of mine.

Few things are more disappointing for a dutiful parent than to have a special event or holiday unwelcomed by the child with, "This is boring. I want to go home." Adult friends who keep bringing only *yesterday* to their relationships often watch their friendships wane. Every day in my office I see couples in therapy who are boring each other toward the death of their marriage.

And God. Can God be bored with us? My poem says "yes" if God is paying attention to us at all. How can we, God's incredible creation, be content to bring our simplistic faith, actions, thoughts, prayers and other trite expressions of our lives as dull offerings to God? Jehovah of the Old Covenant became enraged with unacceptable offerings. Here, in contrast, I only suggest that God is bored. Bored with our begging, complaining moods; our willingness to bring leftovers to the altar; our trite, folksy prayers; yet another "meeting" instead of transfigurative encounters; our plans and programs void of vitality. I have heard church-board members laugh at the double entendre of their office — board member.

Having everything, we still beg, whine, complain for more: more health when we have been profligate, more time at the end when we have been wasteful, rescue from the pit when we have walked carelessly. How about these new entreaties instead: What more is needed? How else may I serve? Who is my neighbor? Enough of our boring begging!

It will take imagination to bring new offerings to the Creator of the New Covenant. The Psalmist prayed, "Create in me a new heart, O God, and renew a right spirit within me." Ezra Pound said that true literature is writing that is new and remains new. Only poor acting can make Shakespeare boring. Only lazy disciples bore God, which may be one of our worst sins of all. In fact, if boring God were confessed as a sin, the church might awake and be renewed. Also, I wonder if God can even be bored with unmitigated saintliness that plays it safe and worships "goodness" — not, I think, David's problem, or Peter's or even Mother Teresa's.

Sure, I know, God loves us all, even bores. But we should at least have the grace to avoid the limelight. Sometimes I even wonder about these poems.

Boredom is contagious.

If God Is the Lowly Ant

If God is the lowly ant
    moving in a broken path
    along that imaginary straight line
    from birth to death,
    searching for life at my table,
    running along as only he is able,
    then a pause
    for something intimate . . .
    the way ants whisper to each other
    of their dead and dying;
If God is the lowly ant
    planting the soil,
    taking tiny seed and corpses to feed
    those seed underground,
    toiling without a sound of weeping,
    keeping hard at what God does best,
    clearing the earth
    with harvest
    and planting for new birth;
I would then, God, ask
    that when you find me on your way
    and whisper last to me,
    stinging me also into your silence,
    you will know me as your own wounded,
    needing of you
    only to be carried down among the seed.

Over the years I have been fascinated by two great galaxies of tiny insects, satellited, colonized and programmed for work. "Busy as a bee" describes both. Bees are mentioned in Scripture, but Proverbs chooses the ant to warn us with, "Look to the ant, you sluggard," as a guard against laziness. Honey is nature's sweet par excellence, and along with milk, God's symbols of the Promised Land. The bee enables life by pollinating flowers. The ant, at the other end of the line, is earth's undertaker. I have been stung by both.

The ant poem came out of a strange and arresting event of childhood when I spent part of a lazy summer afternoon on my elbow peering into the cone of an anthill, trying to imagine their deep dark maze as I watched the colony come and go. Three things surprised me: the great weight they could carry, how they seemed to speak to one another when passing and that they seldom moved in a straight line. The first amazed me. The second had me wishing I could understand what they were saying to each other. Finally, on my way back to our house, I tried walking zigzag and doubling back like an ant, and arrived home with my first buzz on, dizzy and a bit disoriented, confused as to what was happening to me.

That night, before sleep, I recall saying for no reason I knew, "Thank you, God, for letting me walk home like an ant." I had trouble falling asleep. My senses were charged, heightened. I was deep inside myself, while at the same time profoundly connected with everything not me. The darkness was friendly. I felt totally alive. I knew I had experienced a new feeling about God and me — beyond Bible stories and bedtime prayers — and I was sleeplessly joyous with a tiny eek! muffled in my throat.

Years later in England I remembered my walk with the ants when I discovered the craziness of a maze meant to trick and trap, along with its fraternal twin, the labyrinth, which is a single long circuitous path that entirely covers a given terrain. Both are designed for various experiences, the best being to give the soul a healing walk through twists and turns, like life, into the centering presence of God, so that despite all our fits and starts, we finally arrive at God. Sometimes the most helpful thing we can do is to trust the truth of that path, that dizzying joy.

If God Is That Awful Cry

If God is that awful cry
    from the cross,
    Jesus lamenting, "Eloi, Eloi,
    lama sabachthani,"
    rejected, abandoned,
    without hope,
    by God
    who claimed all of him,
    even his death;
Then,
    God is there
    not just with him
    but as present as that cry itself
    when all creation
    is hung up to die
    and the only place
    for God to be
    is so close to Jesus
    as to appear absent
    everywhere else.

The Sixth Word from the cross is the most terrifying moment in the Christian story. This Son of God, as man, was dying in utter despair. After a life of faith and devotion, in the face of death, Jesus Christ, Son of God, Savior, could not find his Father. Quoting the Psalmist, who also experienced unmitigated absence, Jesus pleaded, "My God, my God, why hast thou forsaken me?"

He cried out confessionally for all to hear. His mother and the other women, believers who had followed him to Jerusalem and all the way to the cross, were there, along with his disciples, whom Mark later described with a stabbing indictment when he said, "And they all fled." Finally, his taunters stood by, teasing, "Others he saved, himself he cannot save." In their faces Jesus accused God of abandoning him.

What total devastation Jesus must have felt. His ministry over, his disciples terrified and ready to run, and now a final, great mocking event. God gone! A vacuum! Heaven and earth empty! "Even you, my Father, even you!"

For me, these always seemed the most awful words Jesus ever spoke. I loved his willingness to share our despair in the face of death and his courage to declare it. Yet, it also seemed that Jesus was expecting something more of God that day that he was not getting — something so precious that its absence was equal to the absence of God himself. Did Jesus feel God had let him down by allowing his crucifixion? Was there doubt all along, and now "all this" seemed to say that God was not in his work after all? Was this a collapse of Jesus' belief in his calling? Surely it was more than Jesus feeling lonely, unsupported or ignored. This was a profound absence. At the great redemptive event of history, God was missing.

Might this poem suggest another possibility? Could it be that God the Father was so close, so present, so identified with his son that even Jesus could not see him, could not distinguish that Holy Other? Could it be that Jesus was becoming the Christ that day? The resurrection body was being ordained. God was truly in Christ, as Saint Paul says, completely, triumphantly, eternally. We thus come to the Seventh Word with Jesus in utter surrender to his own glory as he is delivered from despair into life eternal for himself and for us all when he finally says, "Into thy hands I commit my spirit." It is done! Now they are one. "I am in the Father and the Father in me." All margins are dissolved.

If God Is This Last Snowman

If God is this last snowman
    before spring,
    rolled and raised in the image of man
    standing now in my dead garden
    like frozen Adam looking lost,
    trying to recall the names
    of plants withered under snow,
    animals burrowed in,
    birds flown;
Then,
    I will wait
    for the sun to come
    and melt us both,
    him down to bulbs and roots,
    me out-of-doors
    into the waking garden
    where I will watch
    for signs of those
    returning to this place
    as though called,
    even though not one of them
    knows its name.

"... And subdue the earth." This is an early expression of an evolving Jehovah — a God of total autonomy who condescended to share power with Adam and Eve. The price was their obedience. Adam's task was to name the flora and fauna. Naming is an expression of ownership, a station of superiority. Jehovah was sharing ownership and power with Adam.

Thus all creation is named and renamed. Many plants and creatures have multiple names, both scientific and sentimental. But this poem suggests something beyond the notion of ownership by naming. With winter's melting, our garden is renewed, the plants, animals and birds return to replenish the earth as though Adam called. But even if we plant and prune, feed, breed and protect, calling them back to the garden, they come not knowing either their names or even that we called.

We seem to want to command the creatures and the garden itself to yield what we want. We should simply cultivate the garden. They come by invitation only: "Come and see this beautiful place we are preparing for you." If we protect and nurture the garden, they will keep returning. If we neglect, abuse, subdue, then all is lost in the polluted heavens above and the ravaged earth below. And then we are in hell.

After listening to a pro-and-con panel discussion regarding the outlook for our planet, I wrote this quatrain:

OUTLOOK

Looks like our hope for a rainbow is out,
Earth and sky are flooded and dark
And new gods of ruin come mocking our doubt,
Arriving in an empty ark.

If God Is a Butcher

If God is a butcher
    with a block full of blades,
    his nature is to butcher,
    leaving blood lines
    thin as a surgeon's
    along trembling throats,
    as ritual knives
    separate sheep from goats;
If God is a butcher,
    it is his nature
    to purge his ranks
    with a military laser
    swift as the razor
    in the hand-to-hand combat
    of righteous hate
    in creedal debate
    until prodigals believe, or lie . . .
    or die;
If God is a butcher,
    the argument is done,
    all holy wars are won,
    for either we now know
    whence evil comes
    or there is none;
If God is a butcher,
    all we, like altar sheep,
    are gored
    and hung upon a hook,
    as was our Lord.

The Sunday School lesson that Sunday was from the 18th Chapter of I Kings, which tells how Elijah slaughtered 400 prophets of Baal. We students had a Quarterly of thirteen lessons that summarized each Sunday's story and drew a simple lesson. I usually read my lesson on Saturday night after my bath, because of our teacher's first question on Sunday after his prayer. If you could not raise your hand to his "How many of you...?" you were shamed with a look.

The lesson that Sunday was awful enough, but when I read it the night before, the butchering seemed anchored far enough back in history not to be alarming. Besides, this was God for goodness sake.

In class our teacher surprised me with a kind of glee, as with voice and body language he all but reenacted Elijah's success over the pagans. All eight of us boys were stunned by the performance. Finally, it stopped and our teacher waited. Nothing. Then one child, small and dark, shook the room when he said, "My daddy is a Jew who got saved at Dr. Appleman's revival. My mother is a Baptist and she made him come, but he still won't go to church with her. He says Jehovah is too bloody, and he doesn't see how anybody can worship him." There was an awful silence. Then our teacher, whose name I still remember, leaned forward clutching his Bible to his chest and with a low, restrained, raspy voice and a full red face said, "Young man, your daddy is still not saved by the blood of Jesus if he believes that way." The child was startled and began to cry quietly as our teacher started lecturing him on God's plan of salvation, begging the boy to fall on his knees and accept Christ. He still had not done that when the bell rang, and we had to go to closing assembly. The teacher remained in the room with the boy.

In a few months the entire Sunday School turned out for a recognition day ceremony honoring our teacher, who was retiring after thirty-five years of "bringing hundreds of boys to the Lord." He was honored as a great teacher. He got results. Sitting there, I remembered again that Sunday of Elijah's triumph over the priests of Baal. Aaron never returned to our class.

If God Is the Great Lollapalooza

If God is the Great Lollapalooza
      leading the Angelic Bazooka Band,
      lite, tinnish and mostly bland
      down here awaiting heaven . . .
      some of their antics
      with that Spike Jones rig
      can still be forgiven
      if I keep in mind
      who's doing this gig;
If God is the Great Lollapalooza,
      trying to be helpful by suspending
      some of the normal rules,
      such as the writ of habeas corpus
      at the tomb or facts-before-faith
      when betting your life,
      or a better world demands better people —
      fundamentals like that,
And leaving us with fits
      of foolishness called faith,
      disciples accused of body-snatching
      or other schemes that attempt to turn
      nightmares into dreams,
      along with a local god-squad
      that looks like the rest of us
      except they think they are the best of us,
      since they are born again and again
      and again if need be,
      having been forgiven any deceiving
      by only believing;
But,
      if God is the Great Lollapalooza,
      I still expect to ask some day,
      and so may you:
      Is this any way to run a zoo?

This poem and the next one following are among many I have written as cries of the soul on the edge of chucking it all as too ridiculous for belief. One poem ends with a variation on the cliche complaint my father used in the face of some bureaucratic foolishness: "Is this any way to run a railroad?" It may have been the bureaucracy of the government, the local bank or some ruling of the deaconate.

The second poem ends with much more than mere resignation. The last lines proclaim that even if it is all like a circus fantasy world, what a great trip this has been, and "Oh, that majordomo, I shall dream of him forever."

Still, on Sundays and a few other days it all seems too absurd for words. Yet, I keep trying to find just the right words to express those dark feelings. They address the paradox Saint Paul spoke of in First Corinthians when he said, "The foolishness of God is wiser than men." It is in this rational darkness that Christians find irrational light. Jesus said, "He who would save his life must lose it." It is as though we must be able to accept, even embrace, that darkness before we can find and nurture the light of our faith in Jesus Christ.

I awoke one morning from a dream in which I was closing a sermon with these words, "God's most courageous act of all is to trust us with love." God is the love Christ gave to us...openly with healing, obscurely in miracles, mystically in bread and wine, personally with his death. "Greater love has no man than this...." The clown moves in, through and around the other circus acts. Adults often overlook the clown while watching action in the big ring. Children follow the clown who fires their imagination and creates great memories. Unless we become as little children, Jesus warned, we cannot experience the kingdom. And thus we find the root of faith that overcomes the world, even the absurd world of paradox and mystifying contradiction. Doubt is the night that yearns for the light of faith's candle — small, flickering though it may be.

A good friend once sent me a Christmas card from Germany. I now have it framed and hanging in my study. It reads:

In Ihm war das Leben
und das Leben war das Licht der Menschen.

"In Him was life and that life was the light of humankind," says John. Light is perhaps the single greatest symbol we have for God, and the light of faith often shines brightest in the darkness of nagging doubt.

If God Is a Clown

If God is a clown working the crowd
   of this three-ring circus
   and letting himself be chased around
   by a toothless old tiger called Satan,
   and, with a single stroke
   of his paper-tassel whip
   and a puff of smoke, he makes Satan
   magically disappear through a trapdoor
   into the hell of a sawdust pit;
If God is clowning with me,
   setting me on his knee
   and with lollipops and balloons
   telling me that all is well,
   only to drop me
   through that same trap door
   into a hell of merely dying;
If, indeed, God in Christ is clowning,
   setting reality on its ear
   with a Gospel hard to hear
   that the weak are strong,
   the meek inherit the earth,
   and with faith in him and new birth
   even death means life eternal,
   only to let me sleep that great sleep
   forever . . .
Well then,
   what a circus this has been,
   and how I've loved
   the lions, tigers and bears,
   the dancing elephants and calliope,
   even the bazooka band
   and the high-wire acts
   with all those shining faces looking up;
But, oh that majordomo,
   that solitary clown
   who loved us children so,
   who soothed our fears
   and made us laugh with joy to tears
   and feel loved . . .
   I shall dream of him
   forever.

Since the previous meditation speaks for both of the last two poems, I want to offer here a favorite poem from my book *Bruised Reeds*. Perhaps, like a descant above the two preceding poems, it suggests our clumsy child's play at discounting God and Christ and dismissing the Christian community called church, ecclesia, Body of Christ.

MYSTERY PLAY

Lord,
this cup
came down through the years:
Mother, Grandmother,
and a couple of other generations
before them
used it to measure
flour and sugar.
Mother spoke of trying
to take her first dose
of castor oil in hot coffee
from this cup.
I planted a single hyacinth
in it last fall
and kept it hidden
in the cellar all winter.
This spring I took it out
and set it in the sun,
where it grew and blossomed
into a fragrant, lovely thing
that caught the eye
of my two-year-old
who loved it from the window
to the floor.
The cup is broken,
the flower bruised and torn.
The church is that cup,
Christ that hyacinth,
and I am that child.
Amen.

Part Four

If God Is Running Water

If God is running water,
  first blood of all creation,
  dripping now from pipe and faucet
  rising like a mantis
  praying for rain
  at a village watering spigot
  in Ethiopia;
If God is running water,
  diving as the falls at Victoria,
  or creeping through the cracks of sewers
  in crumbling cities everywhere,
  or Old Faithful spouting predictably,
  or dropping from the sparkling black brow
  of a diamond miner in South Africa;
If God is that awful tide that runs
  against the polluting affairs of man,
  water splitting the Red Sea,
  water issuing from the rock under Moses' rod,
  water swaddling Jesus in the Jordan,
  water that is most of the blood of the Lamb,
  water seeping into the sod
  at the foot of the cross;
If God is water coursing through my body,
  then I am a desert,
  and she is my oasis soul fed by her spring,
  growing and spreading
  as my last hope
  under yet another burning day
  of cloudless skies.

It always intrigued me that the Passion story mentions that after the centurion pierced Jesus' side, blood and water issued forth, as though the Gospel writer was not content to mention the obvious but needed to include notice of the presence of water at the crucifixion. Earlier, when Jesus cried out for water, a soldier lifted up vinegar in a sponge to his lips.

Water was such a presence in Jesus' life and ministry: the water of his baptism, the great River Jordan, the Sea of Galilee, where he found the sons of Zebedee, where he sailed and fished with his disciples and performed miracles. And there is his own metaphor of himself when he said, "I am the water of life; he who drinks of me shall never thirst." Jesus said to Nicodemus, "Unless one is born of water and the spirit, he cannot enter the kingdom of God." Water was a synonym for spirit in Jewish thought. They were mixed creatively because of both the unique differences and the clear deference to the power of each to focus the soul's dimensions. Both are deeply inward: breath and water are body's first needs.

Baptism, with its cleansing, burying-and-raising symbolism, has always been the church's rite of passage into the family of believers. Even a drop of water In His Name, even saliva on the finger of the baptizer making a cross on the believer's brow, is enough.

When I was administering the sacrament of baptism in a small New England church in the late 1950s, an African-American mother and her two children were among those presenting themselves one Sunday. It was an American Baptist Church whose practice is immersion. The black family appeared wearing bathing caps. Innocently, I asked if they might remove the caps, and the mother said with a smile, "Pastor, you all don't want to see us with wet hair."

There were only whites in our congregation. These were the first new black members to appear in that loving church family. And I have often wished that all of us that day could have witnessed their hair wet from baptism and rejoiced together beside those healing waters with the Spirit "descending like a dove" upon their radiant heads.

If God Is a Circle Closing

If God is a circle closing,
    reaching around wide like a lover's
    all-embracing arms,
    hands now fingertips apart,
    needing only to touch
    to make all things complete,
    brokenness healed,
    left hand finally knowing the right,
    alpha reaching omega;
Then I pray
    that the hiatus of God's hands
    might not yet close,
    for it is in that awkward place,
    the space between her hands,
    just small enough for me to hide,
    where the breach would be bridged,
    that God grows my soul.

I was quite young when I first saw a picture of Michaelangelo's painting of God and Adam reaching out their fingertips toward each other. I asked my mother: "Why aren't they touching?" Her answer was the response of one living as she believed "in the fear of God." And so she said, "Because Adam would die if God touched him."

"Like burned to a crisp?" I asked.

She smiled. "Maybe like the man and his horse under a tree hit by lightning," she said.

That made sense. "So they never will touch," I said, answering my own questions.

"No," she answered, in the simple direct confident way she had with religious questions.

"Oh," I said, and opened the *Sunday School Quarterly* to the lesson for that Sunday.

I didn't know the artist's genius for leaving space and creating a dynamic tension in the stretching, reaching, almost touching of an awful desire to connect. Some years later in a physics class when the professor connected a battery post to either end of two carbon rods and kept moving their points closer until an electric arc jumped across the open space, then I *saw* the energy. Suddenly I remembered the picture. It was the same between God's and Adam's fingers. Perhaps something of great art is in the part left to the imagination. Perhaps this is also true of our spiritual experience: It happens in the space of "not quite" where *open* means life, energy, growth and possibility — the arc of connection. When do I reach out? How does God reach back? Do I recognize the energy between us? What do I do with that energy? How does it fuel my spiritual life? It happens to me when I reach out expecting God to be there...reaching back.

This often happens during prayer. I imagine reaching out to empty space, not touching God. Then across that hiatus God responds as subtle as neural energy across synapses, and connection is made in an answering moment when new, creative messages come, often having little to do with my request, thank God.

If God Is This Smoky Fire

After Eye Surgery

If God is this smoky fire
    in the cave of my right eye,
    this flame darting, flirting
    with the wet sparkle of walls
    wanting the flare of spring's
    daffodil and forsythia yellows,
    pear whites and tulip tree lavenders,
    settling now as though in the dead
    of winter for shades and shadows,
    snow-glare, early dark,
    driven back inside
    to the ashy, leftover coals of winter
    in the first week of spring;
Then,
    be here with me in this cave, God,
    my back to trickling walls,
    feet to your fire's soft glow,
    and let us talk until morning;
    and perhaps in your burning
    will be the fire I need
    to set this place ablaze with light
    to last this winter of my darkness,
    through this sad season
    until the fountain fire of summer.
Speak, God,
    for you are in this catacomb with me,
    and we only leave together.
If I don't go, neither do you,
    and if I leave, we go rejoicing.

My myopic eyes have required glasses all my adult life. Clues first came one night when I was searching for a movie theater with two other freshmen new to Wofford and Spartanburg. They not only saw the marquee before I did, but could read the titles. Quickly sensing my crippling, like wolf cubs they taunted me as we approached: "Now can you read it . . . NOW?"

Weeks later, I was wearing my father's rimless style of glasses, and the student slowly becoming my best friend was saying, "Gosh, they're ugly. I hope they help your eyes, because they really hurt mine." Next, he began plying me with articles on eye exercises and tales of miracle cures from liniments to Lourdes. I told him I prayed daily for my eyes. He shook his head in disbelief. "At least get horn-rims," he hounded.

Fifty years later, I awoke one morning with what seemed like a drawn shade over my right eye. I panicked and called my ophthalmologist, who had me in surgery the next day, including laser treatment on the left retina not yet peeling off. Good things also arrived with these terrors, one of which was warning my brother who was able to protect his sight with laser surgery.

My poem was written with feelings of rage, resentment and a warning to God left over from a tantrum after panic. I felt caved-in, lost in a new wandering, sightless in Eden. I played all the chords from Samson to Milton, whose sonnet I had memorized that same freshman year, to Helen Keller, in a desperate search for if-they-can-I-can assurance. My vision remains diminished.

An introvert, I have always spent a lot of time not only behind glasses, but even deeper inside. Here I vent these feelings like a stranger in a changing landscape without a white cane. I could hear my friend say, "Poor baby, you'll live."

Then I heard Carl Jung saying, "Go out on a clear night and search the heavens. Now close your eyes and realize it is just as vast inside." And often as heavenly, friend!

If God Is Tree Roots in Our Garden

If God is the great tree roots
   of Oak, Elm, Ash and Sweet Gum
   burrowing deep in our garden,
   which like their branches above
   decide to seek the sun
   and slowly begin rooting upward,
   shouldering loose the stepstones
   across the lawn
   laid long ago and meant to stay,
   now making my way impassable;
Then,
   I accept the message
   and leave the stones raised
   like unsettled grave markers
   to remind me that God
   may move slowly to undo
   all my familiar stepping stones,
   telling me to make new paths
   with nothing more to mark the way
   than the trail I leave
   with my own faint dewprints
   on the grass.

Beloved trees had spoiled our walkways. Sidewalks in the neighborhood were in such upheaval that one could hardly walk without watching for toe-trippers. Walks laid long ago were now hard to navigate. To replace the walks often meant cutting roots when even whole trees could be lost: our green friends who breathe in what we breathe out and give back precious oxygen.

In therapy we use the "draw a tree" exercise as a projective device because trees are such provocative metaphors for humans. A man I was working with was surprised after he drew a tree floating in air, and I asked, "Where are the roots?" "Roots?" he asked. "Yes," I said, "There's the other half, another whole tree underground." Reflecting on his own rootlessness proved insightful for him.

We like laid-out paths, and scouts who go before us leaving markers, even stepping stones. But then we consider those who invaded the wilderness, marched off into the unknown, and were sure enough of their route for us to want to follow. No learning to walk on water here. And few second chances. They either walked or sank. Yet, even explorers had scouts. Lewis and Clark needed Sacajawea. Her golden likeness with her child now graces our new dollar.

But now came roots slowly bowing up our stepping-stones. What to do? I was reminded of root-raised gray slabs and headstones in an old, abandoned New England graveyard. A wreck of a church lay nearby. Children in our group were trying to stay balanced while walking on them. One of us called them off and explained that gravestones should not be walked on. "Couldn't, if we wanted to," one child countered as they all scampered away.

This poem wants to suggest that God keeps uprooting our pathways, giving us a chance to imagine a new way, with nothing left to guide us back but our own footprints in the dew. But why plan to return? And is much of the idea of leaving stepping-stones for others merely our ego inflation? The Gospels say that Jesus walked on water, wrote in sand and spoke of the wind's whimsy as he taught Nicodemus.

Yes, I know that Jesus said, "I am the Way." Still, I must choose to go with him. And the shepherd only carries lambs. Grown-up sheep walk. I may wander and get lost, but still I must find my own difficult path each day on my own all the way home. And Heaven help me if I keep trying to walk on the old stones that God, at the roots, lovingly unlevels.

If God Is a Rising Like Yeast

If God is a rising like yeast,
    a curve and roundness
    against the flat line of death,
    a soaring,
    a rainbow, a child's kite
    sent aloft
    to see it all,
    a weather balloon ball
    set free at sea;
If God is a rising out of the desert
    at Sinai,
    or even if God should be
    Vesuvius erupting in bone-gray ash,
    or ropes of smoke over Auschwitz,
    or mushroomed above Hiroshima,
    any lifting of wings;
If God is a rising birth-star
    in the East,
    the sudden standing up of twelve
    after their simple feast
    as one goes out to die,
    a man hanging on a cross
    under an empty sky,
    an Easter rising then
    and now again in my stony heart;
If an ascending God
    is my own soul's leaven,
    and my Jacob's ladder
    to wholeness called heaven,
    I climb,
    I climb,
    I climb . . .

I find it hard to believe that in my long chain of regrets, I cannot find one I should have pursued until death. I have searched each link for the forger's mark of eternity, and not one abandoned cause, job or relationship, treasured as it was, now seems to be something I should have saved to the end. Elizabeth Bishop's marvelous poem "One Art" reminds us that losing precious things need not mean disaster.

I know a woman who was caught on her cross-country ski trek in a raging Colorado snowstorm. Alicia is sure that she survived only by crying out the names of her children with every slogging step. Ah, perhaps if that had been my strategy! If in the most desperate instances, I had urged myself on with precious names, even Jesus Christ Lord Savior, as some have and do, perhaps then I could have pressed on. But no. Each failure lies like a species that failed to adapt, fossilized at various levels of my memory.

So why drag the chain of regret? Let it go! How good to recall forsaken enterprises and find none wanting a better effort. Why indeed? Because I escape these single regrets by one that speaks to all of them. It is the saddest of all, and the one I need most: my regret that it took so long to see the truth and stop. Such energy, time, love given before it dawned on me, as Frost says, that the ladder was against the wrong wall all along.

And right there is grace. To forgive ourselves as we forgive others for letting *us* go. To forgive ourselves for all those efforts we made with all our hearts only to see the mirage fade. To accept the ache of emptiness, feel the failure and still find the will to quit, leave, climb down and move the ladder so we might climb up again, for a new vision of what the vista beyond the wall might yet be. That is resurrection, perhaps?

It is a basic law of nature that some things must die so that other things might live. So it is our nature, too. And God's.

If God Is Content in His Own Forming

If God is content in his own forming,
    and recalls in a redemptive time
    what contrasts we also carry, and lets
    our quest lie down with questions
    beneath his anointing hands;
If God is content in his own forming,
    blessing each of us apart or near,
    allowing every soul its own journey,
    now needing none to worship him
    or fear his hand;
If God is content in his own forming,
    confessing hunger for our trust,
    wanting our faces to light his darkness,
    yearning to rest within our graces
    though we be slipping from his hands;
If God is content in his own forming,
    and rising to the names we gave him,
    I wait for him to find his voice
    in some new sound beyond commandment,
    pure as the praise of our clapping hands;
If God is content in his own forming,
    I'm content to embrace my own,
    and accept his half-life, half-death gift
    as Christ did at his lonely going out,
    and deliver my own still-growing doubt
    into God's still-forming hands.

Part of my doctoral program was a chaplaincy internship at the University of Chicago Hospitals. One of my patients was an old man who had escaped the ovens of Auschwitz. He had also recently survived two major heart attacks and what he called "a code blue attack with the heart hammer."

Late one night his favorite old aide was completing her routine at his bedside when he suddenly whispered, "I'm going to die now. Would you hold my hand?" Of course she did, while reaching for the call button with her other hand. He grabbed for her arm but she succeeded, and soon the code blue attack was underway. Despite extraordinary effort, he was pronounced dead.

Later the aide wept quietly as she told me her story. In the chaos of Chicago in the late sixties, I was especially moved. "Chaplain, I'm sorry he died, but I'm glad he wanted to hold my hand. First man ever asked me to do that, you know. And him being a Jew and all, too. I think we liked each other. I know I did. He had to have a hard life, but he never complained. Oh, he'd speak up if his food was cold or if I was slow answering his bell. But mostly, he was nice to everybody. Did you know he was a prisoner in the war? He showed me his numbers once. 'Course they were there for all the world to see, if anybody wanted to. Sometimes I wish I didn't code him. He looked so hurt with me. Just rolled his eyes and went to sleep. Then the team came and shooed me out. They just about had to pry his hand loose from mine. It was so soft. I was surprised. Chaplain, I hope God likes him 'cause I did. But I bet he'll tell God a thing or two when he gets there. Yessiree, he won't be one to sit and rock. God will know he's there all right." She laughed. "Anyway, God's got some listening to do now." She laughed again. "Some old man, that one. A real stitch."

If God Is This Living Moment

If God is this living moment,
 this one — now and now and ever now,
 without memory or history
 or time moving away into artifacts,
 moments caught in the mind's need
 to fix itself somewhere in the flood,
 measured not by clocks,
 calendars or carbon
 but in one full moment of knowing — now!
If God is this living moment,
 empty beyond now,
 with no future, no grand plan
 or map, but just light enough
 for the space to the end of sight,
 eye-speed to that star,
 no more, no less,
 not a maybe or what if, but indeed
 a now where I keep breathing God
 in, never out;
 the going out is me dying, becoming then,
 and there and once,
But God enters now,
 God only enters now,
 and now,
 and Now!

The immediacy of God is primal to the great numinous moments of change in the experiences of our spiritual leaders: Abraham leaving Haran, Jacob at Bethel, Moses before the Burning Bush, Jesus at his baptism, Paul on the Damascus Road, Augustine in the garden, Luther posting his Ninety-five Theses at Wittenburg, Pascal with his flame, Wesley strangely moved, Joseph Smith and his tablets, Buddha under the Bo Tree, Muhammad in his cave and others for whom the NOW-moment meant a radical, new God-consciousness. We too have experiences when the presence of God is transforming. Such events may become spiritual milestones from which our lives are forever measured in a before-and-after awareness. For me, one such moment arrived in the Great Mosque at Cordoba, Spain.

Yet this poem says something more. It asks us not only to remember and celebrate the great times of God's appearance among us, but to expect God *now* in any moment, no matter how routine. In our breathing, this breath. In our seeing, this face. In our hearing, this voice. In our feeling, this joy. In our yearning, this touch. In our passion, this kiss. In our hope, this sunrise. In our sleeplessness, this star. To be *alive* is to be in God.

My grandmother, Katherine Molton, had a morning ritual of holding her Bible on its spine and allowing it to fall open between her hands. She then closed her eyes, touched a verse with her finger, and that was her message from God for the day ahead. I once asked her what happened if her finger landed on a passage of "begots." She laughed and said, "I guess I'd just give thanks for all my children and grandchildren." She had eight sons and daughters.

St. Augustine had a similar experience on the day of his conversion. After a long and arduous struggle with his soul, he was in his garden weeping with anguish when he heard a child at play chanting over and over, "Take up and read, take up and read." In Book Eight of his *Confessions* he tells how he randomly opened the Book of Romans where Paul says, "Not in rioting and drunkenness, not in chambering and wantonness, not in strife and envying; but put on the Lord Jesus Christ, and make not provision for the flesh, in concupiscence." He said he could read no further, nor did he need to, and he was converted on the spot.

Aristotle concludes his essay on rhetoric with this rule: "In order that the end of a speech may be a peroration and not an oration, the most fitting style is that which has no connecting particles." The example he gives is: "I spoke, you heard, you know, decide."

However the message arrives, we know it as God's truth, and need only answer.

If God Is This Spinning Mound of Clay

If God is this spinning mound of clay,
    moist, malleable to my touch,
    awaiting my heart's vision,
    going with my need
    for God to be for me
    uninherited, unknown,
    God's own mystery emerging now,
    here, even as my hands seek certainty
    of place and shape;
And if this God
    in my hands feels
    my palm's slap,
    a kneading, fist-pounding rage,
    or the heartbeat pressure of love
    in my fingers, teasing with tips
    arced against the thumb's deep glide,
    accepting the lost grasp and grip of creation
    ever sliding away,
    always only moments from mud;
Then,
    we shall form
    a red clay cup
    and drink together
    each morning, moved
    by God's need to be emptied
    again and again,
    and my fear of never being filled
    at all.

In other poems, I have approached my need to feel that God joins us in the process of becoming. With the incarnation God truly takes on our condition. God becomes human in Jesus Christ. Out of this central truth proceed most of the other unique features of Christianity. One way to read the Bible is to see God evolving from the eye-for-an-eye God, through the ethics, judgment and love of the prophets to Jesus, who urged us to love more, forgive more, share and give away more, even our coat and cloak and go the second mile with those in need. With his stories of the rich young ruler and the widow making her gift, Jesus said we should, for our soul's sake, give away everything, as he was doing. The God in Jesus was no measure-for-measure God.

This poem, this one little piece of the puzzle depicting "God with us," goes a step further and suggests that in some profound and personal way God and I are creating one another to fit our most intimate soul needs. It says that God and I discover these needs as we mold our experiences of one another and that my spiritual life begins and ends with this dynamic, evolving reality. Others may need for God to be the Rock, Unmoved Mover, the Absolute. Yet, if incarnation means what it says and our very nature is "change," what a moving thought to have God not merely with us in our change but for God to take on our condition and become responsive, as a parent learns and grows because of the child. My poem pictures this becoming-together out of mutual needs, ending with communion that makes each of us complete for that intimate moment.

The image of the potter suggests one of the most artistic relationships between creator and creation. Potter and clay are so utterly connected, one imposing its uniqueness upon the other, neither fully in charge, each open to the movement of the other, both needing one another in order to become. Without clay, there is no potter; without potter, clay is merely soil. This poem tells me once more that metaphors of God are not to be pushed or punished, but prayed.

If God Is This Little Girl

If God is this little girl,
    surely no more than four,
    riding a sea-washed, sanded driftwood pony,
    leaving a stick trail, daddy only steps ahead
    looking back and calling her on
    even as she stops to prance a small circle
    and pauses to leave her own mark,
    so that when I arrive moments later
    I see a crooked cross
    she has left almost centered in her ring;
Then,
    ride on, God,
    moving among the archetypes
    in this young, awaking psyche
    that yearns enough at four
    to make a circle in the sand
    and mark the spot where she awoke
    to a simple cross
    with extended arms.

Awaking is such a daring thing for the soul to do. First, to lie asleep contented in the sphere of Mother before and after birth — the long embrace. Then in one slow unfolding to a delicious moment opening like a rose; or bursting in an instant into air like a frisky young dolphin, we know and know we know and are known. A little girl, after baptism, said, "Now God knows my name." Our soul seeks knowing moments. I am reminded of Elizabeth Bishop's splendid poem "In the Waiting Room," when she says, awaking to a new consciousness "at almost seven":

> But I felt: you are an *I*,
> you are an *Elizabeth*,
> you are one of *them*.

The poem reminds me of little bits of drama caught years ago in family movies, old 8-mm films that include sun blotches, shots of sky and ground with the motor still running while herding people together, and those places where a small child cried, "Let me, Daddy, let me." The people all crooked or headless or unfocused into facelessness, and everyone laughs. Something was always weird. There is hardly one perfect film in the many hours now seldom reviewed.

But there was one time when our daughter Jennifer was very young and our family along with a number of her friends were sledding down the long, fast hill beside the Thames River harbour in Groton, Connecticut. When everyone else turned off halfway down, the camera shows Jennifer start to follow where the rest of us had sidetracked, then suddenly she veers back straight ahead, moving faster now, picking up speed all the way down to the bottom with everyone cheering. One perfect run of film.

We only *recognize* our awakenings if we are aware. But whether she knew it or not — and I believe she did — that day was an awakening for that little girl. A first time not to follow the others. Not to play it safe. Not to quit early. To make a new path. To feel longer the rush of wind and movement. To go on...farther. Whatever. To chose.

And somehow these moments become referenced. A precedent is set that sends out small waves, echoes, vibrations down the years at decision time. "Oh yes, I remember when I ...." We feel again such moments in our lives and use them and are cheered on.

If God Is a Rainbow

If God is a rainbow
    curved like a fertile promise
    over this pregnant earth,
    and there is somehow refracted
    through God's prism eye
    a white light of love
    into a spectrum
    of green spring birth,
    a yellow sunflower youth,
    the hot-red high noon truth
    of midlife
    and a cool-blue tempered old age,
Then,
    let it rain and rain,
    and later,
    when the dove returns,
    I'll want to see
    if this spectral God
    will surprise us with a new show
    of good faith
    down where rainbow
    colors meet
    on the ribbon streets
    of all our empty arks
    downtown.

After spending the summer of 1968 in Chicago pursuing my doctorate, I brought my family up from Kansas City. Dian had just received her master's degree the day of Bobby Kennedy's funeral, and Steve, our firstborn, had graduated from high school early in order to be with us. A long summer would get longer.

We had hardly unloaded our U-Haul when Steve begged his way free to go downtown where thousands were assembling to attend or protest the Democratic National Convention. Sensing the risks, we still knew he had to go. He did and had one of the transforming experiences of his life. He sang duets with Mahalia Jackson, held the mike for Robert Lowell and Senator Eugene McCarthy, and marched beside his heroes with the whole world watching. Later he was held up at knifepoint for his forty dollars. We kept Jennifer close, but David, our youngest, had his first two-wheeler stolen out from under him by a gang he called bike rustlers herding through the canyons of Hyde Park. Mary Dian taught at an integrated school, Harvard St. George.

Later, we returned to Kansas City. By then Jack, Martin and Bobby were slain, and we had seen our city torched. After serving in Korea, I felt compelled to take my students to Washington to protest the war in Viet Nam. We promoted open housing, going door to door. We worked with churches still resisting integration, one even objecting to an after-school program in its indoor gym. A young black leader asked the congregation, "Well, I guess it all depends on whether you want your stained glass windows broken from the inside or the outside." Dr. Alvin Porteous, a member of the seminary faculty where I taught, bought a home in a black community, and his family moved in.

Thirty years later, our city is recovering. There are drug houses, trashy streets, nailed-up store fronts, broken windows and shattered, homeless lives. But some of the grand old neighborhoods are coming back with a new racial mix. Yet this city, like so many across America, still has a hole in her heart. And love still has some deep healing to do. Our church, St. Mary's Episcopal, is old in its timbers but new in its inclusiveness. It stands at the core of the city and offers all it has.

Part Five

If God Is My Tour Guide

If God is my Tour Guide,
   the one who skunked the other gods
   and thunked up the whole trip
   in the beginning...
   the god who sent out all those great fliers
   with romantic photos and lush language
   of exotic, erotic, nude-beach getaways
   in this fabulous Garden of Eden,
   with its one-of-a-kind trees, strange fruit
   and seductive, slithering reptiles
   sure to lure and entrance you;
Only,
   after we get there, God, you jinx it all
   with a walk through the Garden
   in the cool of the day
   in a Sneaky Old-Fashioned Stroll sort of way,
   calling our names like daddy for chores
   until we got lost in this great out-of-doors.
Then,
   suddenly we hear your clear SOS,
   which the whole world knows or could surely guess
   means Save Our Souls, get us out of this mess;
But no,
   like Some Obscene Symbol on a bumper sticker,
   it turns out to be the real logo,
   icon, decal, and motto of the place:
   SOS: SAVE ORIGINAL SIN!
So,
   we are tourists trapped, both now and forevermore!
Well then,
   you can just keep it, God —
   the trees, snakes, apples and all;
   I'll not take The Fall
   for this god-awful goof of yours;
But say,
   can you keep sending those other slick brochures,
   the ones with the pearly gates, angelic harp choirs
   and streets of gold?
God,
   that looks like a trip to die for.

To those who prefer their religion served up like warm apple pie a la mode, divined of sweet fruit of which the cook never missed a single bitter bit of peel nor one seed to crack a molar, I apologize for the hijinks across the page. I meant no offense. Actually, it's a silly poem that deserves reflection.

The Fall is a metaphor at the roots of Christian theology starting with St. Paul, who said in his letter to the Romans, "by the trespass of one, the many died." St. Augustine said that Adam's sin of disobedience was transmitted by concupiscence (theological lingo for lust) and thus through the conjugal act to all of us. That set the stage for centuries of "sex is sinful" and all the awful fallout of such ridiculous thinking. This bleak notion of humankind's fate was lifted somewhat with St. Thomas Aquinas' more optimistic view of our condition. Through some fancy footwork among the options, he managed to separate out a before-and-after Adam, so that it is more a fact of nature that we "sin" than that some originating act fated us to an inherited condition, which we must fix with Christ or go to hell.

Through the ages, the Fall has been debated by the pessimists and optimists in the tradition of this doctrine. It appears that more and more theologians see that original scene metaphorically. It is an allegorical effort to answer some pretty basic questions of why-is-it-that...? At any rate, the Fall has consumed enormous time, energy and gray matter, and created bitter dispute dividing Christians of every ilk for centuries.

This poem is a tongue-in-cheek playful teasing of God about the start-up of our habit of doing what we should not, and not doing what we should, and feeling helpless to know why or how to stop it. The poem ends with a rejection of the Fall explanation, while childishly enough, asking for all "the good stuff," even as we recall Mark Twain's taunt about everybody wanting to go to heaven but not yet.

So, whether or not we humans had a Fall somewhere back there, God knows we are "fallen" from our best wishes, dreams, plans, intentions and fundamental goodness. Beyond debate is our need not so much to find a source as a solution. I have my own mantra, which says: "What do I want, and is it good for my soul?" Two fairly simple starting points. But it is a worthy guide only if I have a worthy standard of what I can want and what is good for my soul. Reflective prayer, reading sacred scriptures from many traditions, meditation and dialogue with others on the Way, and the daily writing out of my struggle as here in these pages — all of these keep me reminded that a long time ago I decided to follow, even if often "afar off," the man from Nazareth, who still shows me more about growing a soul that anyone, ever. With him, even the fallen can rise.

If God Is This Dust Devil

If God is this dust devil
    small twister whirling through our barn,
    lifting hay strands and dung dust,
    skirting horse stalls,
    the lame old mule and guinea hens,
    our wide-horned billy goat finding shade
    and one curious cat on a post
    watching God go;
Then,
    he certainly got our attention
    on this hot Carolina afternoon
    when our whole world stopped
    except for bees and butterflies,
    and spun through this old barn
    just like that,
    in one door and out the other,
    midterm in August,
    early, yet looking
    again perhaps
    for a manger
    where love might be born.

I found this poem on its way to nowhere, except perhaps my wastebasket. In the wake of memory came this tiny imagined twister touching down like a child's top along the ground searching for some morsel of delight.

There was the golden August sun casting through the doors of the open-ended barn as far as it could, inviting this lively creature down the lane and into the dusty aisle of the barn. I followed. And as the animals gathered along the way, as with my dreams, I wondered why I was given this memory fantasy. Just before the end I was saying, "Yes, okay, so what?"

When the unconscious has its way with us, fascinating things can happen. Not only may lost memories be recovered, but connections and focus lead us to new perspectives and understandings. Some of these may turn the day or even a relationship around. We simply need to be open and alert to the moving of this spirit within. Often it takes us on soul trips, routine is interrupted, and we have an epiphany: love revealed even in this place. Love that intervenes can change things, lives, even destinies. Love announced at Bethlehem in a manger.

In a train station years ago, I sat across from an elderly woman who was crocheting. Soon a young woman came in and sat a couple of seats away holding her crying baby. The mother changed a wet diaper, then tried nursing in an effort to satisfy her unhappy child. Nothing worked. Finally, the older woman put her handiwork away and, reaching out her arms, asked, "Do you mind if I try?" The exhausted mother, with one glance, gave up her child into the strong hands of this grandmotherly woman. In moments the child was quiet, and soon asleep. We all shared glances and smiles, mystified at the simple movements of trust and love when we are willing to risk.

Saint Paul reminds us in his first letter to the Corinthians that love never fails. His hymn says that even if we have the gifts of wisdom, knowledge and faith enough to move mountains, we still have nothing unless we have love. Edwin Markham says it this way:

> You drew a circle that shut me out,
> Heretic, rebel, a thing to flout;
> But love and I had a wit to win,
> We drew a circle that took you in.

If God Is Dead

If God is dead,
    not much will change at first.
I will rise before dawn
    as now;
    try for a prayer-poem,
    hope for a small hearth-fire
    in my heart,
    offer one brief jubilate
    and walk leisurely
    through the neighborhood
    to the empty house
    where my soul's friend lived.
There I will wait,
    watch for the hearse,
    a moving van,
    and the FOR SALE sign
    likely to appear.
Later,
    if it does not sell
    but the price is right,
    perhaps I may buy it
    myself and move in.
I always liked God's house,
    the art and organ,
    stained glass and tapestry,
    furniture and carved wood,
    all those empty pews
    where my other friends
    could come and sit
    with me.
Besides,
    if I live there,
    perhaps I shall not miss my God
    in here at heart's home
    at all.

At a time when our children began to have friends stay overnight, I thought it might be helpful to clarify the rules of the household. Finally, I ended my little speech by saying, "Your mother and I own this house. It is our property, with all the legal aspects of ownership. We are responsible for what goes on here and can be held accountable by the parents of your friends. However, this is also your home, our home, and you are free to enjoy yourselves within the real boundaries and rules of house. Just remember," I said, wishing they would smile, "our house, your home." I hoped this simple distinction, wobbly as it was, might help.

When I was a pastor, I heard the same distinctions. A mother of four said, "This is the only place where I get to be alone with me all week." A young father, raised Catholic, often stopped on his way to work and sat alone in our sanctuary, plain, white and Protestant as it was, to meditate. An elderly woman in a nursing home and missing her church, said, "It's the only home I have left. My dearest memories are there: baptisms, weddings, funerals, all the Sundays with John and the kids in a row. The party for our fiftieth was there. Oh my!" We knew a couple who converted an abandoned church into their home. David, our youngest, asked, "Does God still live there?"

There are sacred places throughout the world: from Guadalupe to the Black Hills; from Babiyar to Dachau; from the Acropolis to the Catacombs; from Rome to Fatima; the Taj Mahal to Kyoto, Mount Sinai, Petra and Bethlehem and scores of others, famous in the collective and precious in the personal. These are where we expect to experience the Holy, some movement of the soul taking us to new heights or depths of longing in the soul for love, peace or new life. Perhaps in these places we hear differently.

Yet, might it be that wherever we find ourselves we are on holy ground. We are with Jacob at Bethel. We hear Elijah's "Still small voice." In the mystery of silence something speaks of God. Jesus asked us to seek, listen, find. God wants to speak with us in our soul's home of inwardness, where we are most uniquely and personally ourselves. Go inside. Finding *that* sanctuary can be a great awakening. The seat of the soul is the holy space of eternal meeting. There we may end all our prayers with the psalmist, saying, "and I shall dwell in the house of the Lord forever."

If God Is That Little Boy's Yo-Yo

If God is that little boy's yo-yo
    as he was for me at twelve,
    talking in my dark temple
    with my elders,
    Mother away from kitchen and Bible
    and Dad at home now from his toy-box
    little railroad running
    like a serpent through
    southern pine and swamp,
Home to my bedside for prayers
    and talk of their distant God
    while mine was still doing
    walk-the-dog, taking heads off
    daffodils from my own hand,
    or round-the-world, just missing
    my little brother's head as he sat
    at my feet amazed —
    my God,
    flying up and down,
    out and back, humming the air
    I breathed,
    pounding
    into my palm,
    then taking flight again
    like a bird from my fingers
    soaring up over me
    between heaven and earth,
    visiting as my very own angel . . .
If God is that little boy's yo-yo,
    then God is surely everywhere.

The yo-yo keeps coming back. It cycles in and cycles out, an everlasting toy. It soars in popularity, then plays out, only to return. It would seem that somewhere, every moment, a child is practicing those timeless acrobatics toward a smug assurance of sheer joy.

How far we are today from the kind of entrepreneur who waited years ago near my school yard for the last bell. My magician, my sleight-of-hand artist, was a golden-faced, smiling Hawaiian, his pockets crammed with enamel-smooth yo-yos of every color for only a dime. He dazzled me. His tricks were endless, playing his yo-yo like a circus animal jumping, looping, stretching, hanging mid- air, around and over. Some hummed, sang or whistled through their metal vents. The master kept smiling, holding my trance, always smiling as I nodded into submission and reached for my dime.

I had thrown tops with boys trying to see whose would spin longest, until like fighting cocks our young blood rose and we threw to split the other boy's top. But yo-yos were different. They were versatile, graceful, peaceful, singing their own om-mantra. I adored them, traded and saved to buy yet another with a new decal or sparkle.

I never said, "Look what I can do." It was always, "See what my yo-yo can do." When I rode my bike, skated or played piano, I was in charge. But my yo-yo seemed endowed, autonomous. It embodied its genius and timing, curve and flight, memory and balance, and quiet acceptance of my devotion. I handled my yo-yo like a priest with holy things.

On my first yo-yo Easter, my mother, always gentle, said, "No, son, you can't take the yo-yo to church. That's God's house, and we go there to worship. Now be a good boy."

As she turned to go, I slipped the yo-yo into my pocket.

If God Is Our Love's Last Task

If God is our love's last task,
    he's in our striking clock
    upon that mantel shelf
    leaving its voice upon the air
    like a heartbeat of itself
    resounding everywhere,
    as autumn skies echo the beat
    above in migrant, honking geese,
    and I suppose it will repeat
    in whales singing in fathomless seas;
If God is our love's last task,
    he is with us here
    as we turn toward winter
    and my heart's tolling,
    beats the time
    as we find our parts
    in this archetypal dance
    even as that pulsing star
    reflects the rhythm of our earth
    while setting moon
    and waiting sun hang pendular
    like lamps of death and birth;
If God is our love's last task,
    I listen to my old slow drum
    in this late night of our years
    beating with a tedium
    of encroaching fears
    as death waits
    between each wave
    while heart to heart
    in love we lie
    and pray God each
    will grow in time
    brave enough
    to let the other
    die.

More than once in a dark reverie I have wondered about last tasks, from assembling yet another photo album to giving away my library, from last words to friends and loved ones to some final pilgrimage to a hallowed spot, from choosing who should receive what of my keepsakes to that last "best" poem. The list grows with each musing.

There are now official lists of required last things. A will, a living will, a living trust and power of attorney head the list. The word "living" seems somehow to give buoyancy to this grim task. Jokes begin about shrinking everything into a retirement home apartment. A scholar friend of mine watches all of his precious books, which he often bought instead of food, go at auction for pennies, and is stunned to find how easy it is to let them go. After my mother died, I saw my ever news-hungry father reduced to caring most that the alert device he wore around his neck was working.

I recall my professor and advisor at Yale, H. Richard Niebuhr, saying in 1958 that the next great concern of the church would be teleology, last things, how God's creation would be consummated in its own fulfillment. If our life is so much grief for what we lose — childhood's unconsciousness, the passing of people and things with a growing sense that nothing lasts, the encroaching shadow of death — then a looming awareness of all *last* things ignites anxiety. But also, for some, it can fire imagination. Thus we may move in fantasy from a hell of loss to a heaven of arrival. Last things can be about courage and love, gratitude and sharing. It can take us into our clearest dream of who we are and may yet become. My dear friend and colleague, Tom Green, dying young of a brain tumor, choreographed his last days like an artist, greeting and sharing with those he loved, teaching me so much about how to do life's end. A woman once told me that her father had died in his sleep and she prayed to go that way also. She was surprised when I disagreed and said that I was curious about death, wondered about how I would do my dying and believed I wanted to be alert to the end. "Well," she said, "you may jolly well change your mind when you get there." She may be right, and I told her so.

Watching another take up those last tasks can be heart wrenching. It can also be sacramental, a time to experience grace. If they are going and we are yet remaining, our task may be to have the courage to let them go. Often, if they linger needlessly, it is the one last gift we can give: "I can let you go now. Your soul is free to fly." Lovers know their love does not make them one. Sometimes our love is a blanket that only barely covers our separateness.

If God Is Just One Long Good-Bye

If God is just one long good-bye
    after my beaming childhood meeting
    with her when all seemed welcome,
    only to find that greeting
    slipping away
    and so soon turning into excuses
    for our parting
    with some vague promise of reunion,
    then that last quick waving,
    a salute with a nod to leaving,
    as my hand goes high,
    flagging,
    now both hands sawing
    the air in a crisscross
    with a flourish of
    Wait-up, Don't-go, Come-back,
    then their slow floating descent
    and that last palms-up
    resignation of farewell,
    Godspeed,
    so long . . .
Well, I'm sorry,
    but I'm just not content
    with her good-bye,
    and I plan to arrive
    at the mansion
    in good time,
    and what's more
    I plan to surprise her
    with a front door
    greeting, like . . .
Hello, I'm home.
Is anybody here?
And, depending on the answer,
    you can bet
    that you're invited
    to my best party yet.

"Okay, time to start saying good-bye." Everyone gets hugs and kisses, along with admonitions about driving carefully, sending recipes, remembering to call or write or say hi to someone not there. Mother follows us to the front steps and waits as we do last-minute loading of bags and kids. Dad circles the car a time or two patting and kissing his grandchildren once more, watches us back out, stands in the driveway waving, then in the street, until we are over the hill and out of sight. At family gatherings it always took a while to leave, but the leave-taking is still a powerful part of our memories. Soon there would be another home-going, and still another good-bye.

It often seems that most of what I do as a pastoral counselor is grief work. Indeed, so much of our living deals with the anxiety of leaving — from relatives, friends and animals to relationships with jobs, houses, neighborhoods and even trees. At the height of the Dutch Elm disease we lost four giants that shaded our house and yard. Hearing them fall at their cutting was awful. People report grief over the loss of childhood faith, the seeming absence of God, the emptiness of prayer, a loss of meaningfulness and, finally, the relentless approach of the death that haunts us all. In *The Courage to Be* Paul Tillich says, "Anxiety is finitude, experienced as one's own finitude."

This poem suggests that even if our relationship with God feels like one long good-bye, especially if we experience God-consciousness in all of life, we should not see these losses as God forsaking us. Indeed, we might reframe them to see all leave-taking as a necessary part of our home-going. Our whole journey is a return to our Creator. Without this hope we are lost in one eternal funeral cortege. Among all the other metaphors of rebirth and new beginnings, Easter is God's promise and our hope for a joyous home-going. *That* faith changes everything.

If God Is My Usable Past

If God is my usable past,
    the part worth saving,
    the minutes, episodes,
    chance encounters
    when I measure the moment
    by soul standard,
    an inward counting
    of worth and meaning —
    the past
    stumbled upon
    or given as an outright gift
    to which I first said no
    then later yes
    with a bless-me-now
    petition of recognition
    instead of my normal
    pitiful why-me pout;
    yes!
    that usable past
    as even bruised fruit preserves
    and shriveling grapes store sweet wine;
Then,
    out of the past, O God,
    let the useless become usable,
    the broken find repair,
    the lost be found
    as when the prodigal's nowhere
    with a change of compass
    becomes now here
    at homecoming.

Many years ago when I first read the phrase "usable past" in an essay by Van Wyck Brooks, I pondered my own history. Recently, when I recovered these words as a metaphor for God, I began to reflect on my soul's usable past, elements in the history of my journey to which I might return for guidance and sustenance: those times when I felt God's sure presence in the life I was making. There were many, some more certain than others. A few that seemed sure of God are now lost in the fictions of youth. Those remaining are precious.

Childhood for all of us is a prefiguring of the adult life. Moments of fear, hope, guilt, forgiveness, love and trust, so startling to the child, become magnets attracting other defining events. Often I am shaken when I look back to see me moving as a child discovering people and experiences that became benchmarks for the growing adult soul. The child is indeed the mentor. Wordsworth was right to remind us that the child is the father of the man.

When I become careless with the utter candor of life, presumptuous and disrespectful of all the child discovered in joy and pain, I am humbled to return to him and thank him for those early epiphanies and promise again to remember and honor the young soul's awful, hard-earned wisdom.

When I was ten and my brother Ellis was six, he fell out of a boat I was rowing. I scrambled to save him. Since neither of us could swim, I'm sure we made a frightful sight. Over the years he has teased me that his "Freudian slip" over the side occurred in the iffy atmosphere of sibling rivalry. At seventy I know that this one small piece of my own usable past demands that I give thanks for him daily and love him to the end.

If God Is Zero-One

If God is Zero-One,
    no-thing and everything,
    both no and yes,
    abyss of awful emptiness
    and plethora blessing,
    cipher and the sentinel 1,
    black hole and all wholeness,
    absolute other and incarnate Christ,
Then, God,
    since I too am one of opposites,
    with faith in your fullness
    and envy of your emptiness . . .
    fill me
    when I am empty of you,
    empty me
    when I am too full
    of myself.

In my own believing, I need God to join me in being unfinished. I speak of this in another poem titled, "If God Is Content in His Own Forming." In Christ, God takes on our condition, our humanity, and for me God's ultimate gift of incarnation is to share our essential nature of being in process, to share growing with us. It seems to me this would be extraordinary grace: not only that we may fail and be forgiven to try again, but that each day, every step of the way, in the next moment a new movement in my becoming may occur, and that God joins me as a "work in progress" — me in my station and God in God's. Two great twentieth century poets, Rilke and Unamuno, speak of God as striving toward God's own completion in creating humankind. Following the philosopher Albert Whitehead, theologians Charles Hartshorne and John Cobb, with their Process Theology, have struggled here.

An arrived God is no great assurance for me. Besides, as I follow God through the biblical journey, it appears that God is evolving toward being more humane and loving, a more decent God. I recall as a teenager saying to a friend, whose God seemed vengeful with threats and punishing with hell, that my father was a better person than his Father God.

A part of my faith vision is of God joining me at every level of my existence, not just side by side, but in it all as God. After the Holocaust, people of every faith, and especially Jews, were asking, "Where was God?" There could be but one answer, "God was there in the camps, in the ovens." God was present in prisoners like doctor Viktor Frankl, who told stories at night to inspire in his fellow captives the will to survive. If we believe God could not stop that horror, but could indeed share it with the doomed, surely we can claim a God whose ultimate caring is to share our greatest hope: that, though unfinished, we are evolving toward ever deeper consciousness of our possibilities as God's creation. Such a God would join us in one of our worst fears — personal change — and what is perhaps our worst disease — obsession with perfection — often followed by great guilt when we fail. When Jesus said, "Be ye therefore perfect even as your Father in heaven is perfect," the Greek word is *teleioi,* which means *complete* rather than our notion of "correct in every way."

A true incarnation would be for God to join us in *becoming* complete. God is Zero, no-thing, and God is One. The spectrum from Zero to One might be seen as God *becoming* with us, through Christ, complete.

If God Is To Be My Last Rite of Passage

If God is to be my last rite of passage,
    dry Camel's Eye,
    Way through Kafka's castle wall
    or Blake's heaven's gate,
    or even Alice's door, for goodness sake,
    last stall-out toll booth
    where I surrender all my brassy tokens,
    pride's pocket change
    picked up along the way
    from seems-like-only-yesterday
    down to that last tight squeeze
    through the needle's eye
    at that vexed exit
    where I could both end
    and begin again;
If God is the slit in the curtain
    that I slip through, certain
    that this adieu to lights
    and bright faces, polite applause,
    cat calls or bravo is but the final pause,
    bow, wave and goodnight,
    only to enter upon a fairer stage
    with familiar faces on the other side
    of this divide;
Then,
    I shall enter quite amazed
    and stammering about how thrilled
    I am to be here . . . there . . . anywhere,
    everywhere,
    at last.

Dylan Thomas, in his splendid poem, "Do Not Go Gentle into That Good Night," begged his father to "Rage, rage against the dying of the light." I hear people say, "It's not death; it's the dying I fear. Getting there, getting it done." Ah, there's the rub.

Occasionally I am taken with how I struggle with the affront of life's transience and with my own search for transcendence. After years of leading worship in non-liturgical settings, I was asked by our rector why I was becoming an Episcopalian, to which I replied, "I am looking for an experience of transcendence which rises a little higher than my own head."

My soul wanted to be lifted by the ancient liturgy itself regardless of my sermon or prayers. The hard press of our transient existence in a natural world, caught in eternal cycles of birth-and-death seasons, gives me a longing to escape through some alluring hatch off any holy mountain into eternal life.

John Donne, the great metaphysical poet who was Dean of St. Paul's Cathedral in London, announced in one of his *Holy Sonnets* as though it were an edict, "Death, thou shalt die." Such confidence. Such authority. Such gall. Such whistling in the dark, some would say. Yet that is why Easter shook the world and Christianity flowed like an incoming tide. We believe death will deliver us over into the hands of a God who welcomes our arrival. So, with faith out of the depths of an oceanic hope, we demand that death become wings into life with God. The poem on the facing page celebrates both exit and entrance, death's passage from here to there, into the holy mystery of all that is beyond.

Once, early in the morning when Mary Dian and I were leaving the Eternal City of Rome, a full milky-white moon was setting in the rear window of our taxi. Through the windshield the sun rose like a coin, a crimson disc, partner to its mate across the sky. "What a perfect ending!" we exclaimed together.

If God Is This Radiant Sunflower

If God is this radiant sunflower,
    eye on earth
    watching here in summer air
    for chorister bees
    and angel butterflies,
    then away
    to mirror vistas of the moon
    and far beyond
    to fields of mandala worlds
    turning on magnetic stems
    in august airlessness;
Then,
    with all saints
    I am blessed
    at last to catch
    a golden glimpse,
    a shining trace,
    of the very face
    of God.

On our summer trips to Rocky Mountain National Park, except for the beautiful, haunted Flint Hills, the only relief from the long flat drive across Kansas was the glorious deep fields of sunflowers. After wheat, corn, beans, pig and cattle farms, suddenly sunflowers. It was as though someone who could see the vast patchwork of the state from above said, "Plant here and here, and over there, yes and beside that great barn. Yes, yes!"

After one such vacation, I promised myself that next summer there would be sunflowers in our garden, even though the great umbrellas of Oak and Ash leave us mostly in shade. But there was one open spot on the remaining stump of Elm where I filled a half-barrel with good soil, and planted three sunflower seeds, expecting to save the strongest. The one I kept soon grew tall and bloomed majestically, becoming a focal point of the garden. One afternoon when our sunflower seemed close to seed, I knew I needed its photograph. There was a slight breeze, and I had some difficulty getting my shot. Finally, when all was in place under the lens, just before I snapped, a huge bumblebee, as though on cue, lit just off center, and I had a perfect sentimental and old-fashioned picture for the album. Never since have I needed to grow another sunflower.

Sunflower poetry is scarce. However, I recall a song popular in our parents' day with lyrics written by the eighteenth century Irish poet Thomas Moore. These lines are the last four in his poem, "Believe Me, If All Those Endearing Young Charms":

> No, the heart that has truly loved never forgets,
> But as truly loves on to the close,
> As the sunflower turns on her god, when he sets,
> The same look which she turned when he rose.

I am taken with the poet's image of constant love captured in the sunflower's faithfulness to its god, the sun, when it set, and following on through the night, turning to face the east again to meet its golden god rising.

In my poem the image changes, so that it is God's face resplendent in the face of the sunflower, reminding us not only of the ancient sun god at the center of our solar system, but also of our eternal God at the heart of love, turning, ever turning, following to find us.

Epilogue

If God Is My First-Seed Myth

If God is my first-seed myth,
    inherited like my eyes and gait,
    timbre of voice and my genetic code,
    and given to me out of my soul's trek
    across the terrain of infinite space
    where she caught glimpses
    of gods, goddesses and my God
    growing like pearls from grains of time...
    glimpses she caught of these gathering deities
    in mirror pools, wet caves, in sun-flakes
    through leaves and mountain mists,
    hollowing trees, flower bells
    and lidless serpent eyes,
    or fluttering away
    even from dropped dung blossoms...
    until my God arrived over time in my mind
    as my own joyous myth,
    giving my backbone buds of nerve,
    my eyes precious glimmerings,
    my mouth kisses of speech,
    my heart its own dread countdown pulse,
    my brain memories of lives lived and lost...
    moving here to where
    my soul waits for the new feathering out
    of my own clipped wings,
    watches with other grounded angels
    dreaming of flying,
    and lifts these arms toward God...
Then,
    I am ready to make the long journey back
    to where we began
    with my first flight
    into pure light.

If God Is That Shadow

If God is that shadow
 languishing against the tenement wall,
 cold on a melting day,
 hardly breathing with the old man
 bundled in black, almost twin,
 almost aware
 of the paper bag fluttering at his feet
 like a street dog sniffing and moving on...
If God is that shadow also moving,
 bracing, holding the wall steady
 for the old man struggling,
 then waiting, waiting...
 now crumbling slowly to a crouch,
 then up again, up and swaying...
 surprised,
 wide-eyed awake, sure now,
 standing, but in a bow
 bent with still wanting the grave...
If God is that shadow
 once more,
 slowly peeling down the wall,
 sun dying, shadow fading,
 losing light,
 going as the old man goes,
 huddling down toward darkness,
 seeping down through the iron grate,
 offering the only warmth for both
 as the old man sleeps...
Then,
 attend him well, God,
 all the way to Sheol,
 all the way home.

If God Is This Smokey Crystal Cross

If God is this smokey crystal cross
    strung at your throat
    on its silver chain,
    burning now in slivers of flame,
    dancing to the candle glow
    of altar fire
    as you kneel to pray,
    and suddenly your cross
    in meditative rest
    hangs pendant-like a blade
    above your breast;
Then,
    what's to keep its dagger sheathed,
    knowing as we do
    that a double cross
    hides buried there,
    offering itself as relic
    for a holy kiss after prayer,
    or for your Judas kisses
    on either side
    of your so tender neck,
    with no savior near
    to stanch the flow
    of your precious blood?

If God Is This Branding Iron

If God is this branding iron
 shaped in Celtic cruciform,
 ancient, dusty, flaking
 with bits of curling rust
 and residue of God-knows-what
 singed upon the iron long ago —
 hair, hide, wail of pain
 seared with sign of the cross —
 ranks, legions, village and tribe
 trooping to the iron
 of circle and square,
 forging heaven and earth
 in a martyr's feast,
 taming the soul
 with a sorcerer's fire
 flaming in God's own hand;
Then,
 mark me, God!
 sign my heart with your scar
 so that when I wander
 or am driven scapegoat free
 into the wilderness,
 I may know for sure
 who promised to cure
 my own need
 to name my soul,
 and gave me his.

If God Is Eternal Thou

If God is Eternal Thou,
    not you nor I nor we
    but utterly Other,
    wholly beyond knowing
    except
    as God allows
    along all the paths out and away
    from Thou to me for me to see,
    taste, touch, smell
    all that smarts, soothes, quickens,
    awakens —
God up close
    seeing me touching ecstasy,
    tasting at the elemental core,
    smelling my way like a cat
    to the fecund delicious fruit
    of earth, sea and sky,
    chewing leafy life,
    loving this rising ache of longing,
    arriving prepared to leave,
    dreaming
    against nightmares that haunt
    this weak heartbeat of hope;
    dreaming, always dreaming toward life,
    toward you,
    God,
Thou outloud!
    Listen to that sound
    out of the slumbering skull
    just before first dawn.
Thou!
    How art Thou now,
    now that I know your name?
You are known.
I am mystery.
We are one.

Benediction

God Is

God is a word I peel with my teeth.
God is an idea coiled in my mind.
God is a midwife at birth and rebirth.
God is a voice calling from the void.

God is a feeling setting me free.
God is a warden still searching for keys.
God is a clown laughing at me.
God is the enemy demanding my life.

God is a crossroads at which we part.
God is a neighbor gossiped with friends.
God is a friend I embrace with my heart.
God is a captain who wants his ship back.

God is a scout without compass or map.
God is a dream hassling my sleep.
God is a chalice holding my will.
God is a metaphor of all that is true.

God is a lover claiming my soul.

Acknowledgments

My poems have been in the writing for many years, and these are only a portion of them. During this time many people have been a part of my work. Some have been editors and publishers, some were general readers who shared their ideas and feelings about the poems, and some offered pulpits, lecture halls and classrooms for early readings. Many are old friends and family, who found ways to buoy my spirit, while publishers praised the poems yet reminded me "there is no money in poetry."

I wish I could introduce each of these special people, but the best I can do is list their names as a token of my gratitude. Each one knows why his or her name appears here and how they are remembered at this time in my life. To those who should be included and are not because of my lapsing memory, I invite you to remind me, and I will write you a poem of your own, beginning "If God Is...." You know the rest.

First, I want to express my gratitude to the editors of the following journals who published these poems: *The Christian Century*, *The Catholic World*, *Congregations — The Alban Journal*, *First Things*, *The Journal of Pastoral Care*, *The Ligourian*, *The Other Side*, *Pilgrimage*, *Reflections* (a journal of opinion for Yale Divinity School, Berkeley Divinity School and Yale Institute of Music), *Sojourners* and *Theology Today*.

Then, I want to acknowledge Dean Peerman, recently honored as one of the great editors of the religious press. Soon after beginning his long tenure with *The Christian Century*, Dean was an editor who always gave my poems a good reading, and over many years, he often selected them to appear in this highly respected journal.

I must also mention the place of that beloved poet, the late John Ciardi, in my early years of submitting poetry to journals. Once, while Ciardi was poetry editor at the *Saturday Review* and a professor at Rutgers University, he wrote a long letter to me from Rome while he was on sabbatical translating Dante. He responded with humor and wisdom to my poems and my desire to do graduate study with him. His words bolstered my faith in my own writing, and I took courage in his penciled gentle but critical notes in the margins of the poems I sent him.

Next, I am grateful to Fr. Robert Pagliari, the editor who referred me to Tom Turkle, president of Forest of Peace Publishing, who first suggested that I write meditations to accompany the poems. He and my editor, Tom Skorupa, with loving care, have given this work its public life. I do not know how I could have had colleagues more committed to this effort. They have loved the poems and welcomed each change or new addition up to the last deadline. Tom Skorupa has included me in the discussion of the major decisions that bring a manuscript to book. They made it all happen.

Now, I want to single out my expert readers, who read as editors offering critical feedback that helped shape the book. They are: Jim Carpenter, Harris and Susan Parker, David Barstow, Larry Racunas, Bill Tameus, Bob and Mary Haas, Paul Jones, Bill Malcomson, Kathy Butterfield and Steve Molton. Their personal, sensitive insights were so helpful in the unfolding of this manuscript.

After these, the line lengthens to include members of my church poetry group, friends and family members. Of these, I first want to mention our son, Steve, and his wife, Pamela, who early on made a cassette of theirs and their friends' voices reading and singing the poems. As a birthday gift from all of our children, it brought a different dimension to what I had written and encouraged me toward sharing the poems. Then come Mary Louise Newberry Bohler, Chad Simmons, Bob Price, Mary Hargadon, Steve Walker, Al Porteous, Mary Kay Brooks, Donna Ziegenhorn, Debbie Yeo, Marie Mason, Janice Downey, Terry Schultz, Jennifer Monson, Paul Wenske, Jim Simpson, Bruce Rahtjen, David Brock, Andy Vos, Maryann Werst, John Morrison, Bob Mann, Judith Christy, Mike Shaffer, Catherine Hiller, Sydney Backstrom, Jan Coil, Ann Nixon, Jack Taylor, Blair Hyde, Wendy MacLaughlin, Dorothy Curry, Bette Smith, Tony Beasley, Bob Stewart, Kate Ghio and my brother and his wife, Ellis and Marcie.

Next follow our other children and grands: David and Robin, Jennifer with her son, Eric, and his wife, Becky, and Ethan (our great-grandson), who cheered with us all when word came that Tom Turkle would publish If God Is..., and Aaron, Jennifer's younger son, who offered comments that were always poignant.

One of the most important people in the preparation of this book is a dear family friend, Helga Beuing. She faithfully typed and retyped many morphs and editions and through it all made many helpful suggestions. Her energy and loyalty will always be remembered and appreciated.

I would be remiss if I did not include here the memory of my parents, Hiram Newton Molton and Wilhemina Beatrice Lane Molton. A second dedication might well have been "To My Mother's Voice," as I recall her singing and reading to me during my tenderest years.

Finally comes my wife, Mary Dian, my friend, partner and lover for more than half a century. My poems have gone first into her hands, often only moments after writing. No one has done more to inspire the poems and encourage the making of this book, and I shall be forever grateful.

The Author

Warren Lane Molton holds degrees from Wofford College, Southern Baptist Theological Seminary, Yale Divinity School and Chicago Theological Seminary. He has pastored churches in Washington, D.C. and Groton, Connecticut, served as a military chaplain in Korea and was campus minister at the University of Connecticut during the years that included the Civil Rights Movement and the Viet Nam War. For seven years he was Professor of Pastoral Theology at Central Baptist Theological Seminary and was later an Adjunct Professor at St. Paul School of Theology.

Dr. Molton is director and cofounder of the Counseling Center for Human Development in Kansas City, Missouri. For the past thirty years he has had a full-time pastoral care practice, including individual, couple, group and family therapy. He is a recognized specialist in the field of couple relationships and has authored three books on the subject, including *Friends, Partners and Lovers* and *How Lovers Stay Close.*

He has also coedited a book about the creative church and has authored a collection of prayer-poetry, *Bruised Reeds*, as well as scores of articles and poems in leading journals. Besides being past poetry editor of *Pilgrimage: The Journal of Existential Psychology*, he lectures and leads workshops on adult relational life, and the use of poetry for spiritual growth and healing. Dr. Molton teaches courses in churches and seminaries and also consults with organizations and corporations in their effort to increase awareness of spiritual consciousness in the workplace.

He is married to Mary Dian Molton, a Jungian therapist. Parents of three grown children, Stephen, Jennifer and David, they presently reside in Kansas City and are members of St. Mary's Episcopal Church.